REPEAT

A WARNING FROM HISTORY

REPEAT

A WARNING FROM HISTORY

Dennis Glover

Allison & Busby Limited
11 Wardour Mews
London W1F 8AN
allisonandbusby.com

First published in Great Britain by Allison & Busby in 2025.
Originally published in Australia and New Zealand by Black Inc.

A CIP catalogue record for this book is available from
the British Library.

10 9 8 7 6 5 4 3 2 1

ISBN 978-0-7490-3321-7

Typeset in 11.5/16.5pt Adobe Garamond Pro by
Allison & Busby Ltd.

Excerpt from "Aftermath" copyright © Siegfred Sassoon by kind
permission of the estate of George Sassoon.

Printed and bound in Great Britain by Clays Ltd. Elcograf S.p.A

EU GPSR Authorised Representative
LOGOS EUROPE, 9 rue Nicolas Poussin, 17000, LA ROCHELLE, France
E-mail: Contact@logoseurope.eu

CONTENTS

Part II
FARCE

To Volodymyr Zelensky. Who else?

völkisch – *adjective (of a person or ideology), populist or nationalist and typically racist*

populist – *a person, especially a politician, who strives to appeal to ordinary people who feel that their concerns are disregarded by established elite groups*

– Oxford Languages

PREFACE

Do you ever stop and ask, 'Is it all going to happen again?'
– Siegfried Sassoon, *Aftermath*, **March 1919**

The populists are back. The 1920s and '30s have returned. The first time around, it was all so new. We were taken by surprise, disoriented, knocked off our feet, terrified, cowed. This time we have no excuse. We know the populists' game plan. And we know that unless we show the strength to face them down, disaster will follow. If you doubt me, read on.

In this struggle, history is our friend. The similarities between then and now are clear and unsettling. The same patterns are unfolding before our eyes. To stop them repeating in full, we need to learn the lessons of the past. It won't be enough to rely on others for this knowledge; we must all be historians now. And as citizen-historians our task is simple: to stop the Second World War being followed by a Third. Armed with the lessons of history, we must demand our governments and political parties act strongly and with courage.

Learn, good people. Fast.

INTRODUCTION

Switch on the news channel right now. Does it all look somehow familiar? Ranting populists. Phoney elections. Politicised courts. Attempted putsches. Assassinations. Bullets to the back of the head. Wars. Tank battles. Cities bombed flat. Calls for caution and non-intervention. Angry mobs coming for the Jews, for the Muslims and for sundry 'others'. Facts that are difficult to distinguish from lies. A world of unthinkable savagery. If it looks familiar, it's because you read about such things at school. In history class.

On 6th January, 2021, a thought occurred to me while watching Donald Trump's right-wing vigilantes storm the Capitol building in Washington, DC: perhaps history really does repeat. A clock started ticking in my mind.

Let's go back. It's 1923, and in Munich, a nascent political party, led by a ridiculous street corner agitator named Adolf Hitler, attempts a putsch against the Weimar Republic. It fails. Hitler is arrested and jailed but released soon after by sympathetic judges and politicians, enabling him to run again when the times suit him better. Sound familiar?

Fast-forward ten years. It's now 1933, the height of a global economic depression, and that same easily dismissed nobody has taken power and started dismantling German democracy. The first concentration camp opens, in Dachau. Laughed at and disregarded by all upstanding people, Hitler has the last laugh. The clock ticks on . . .

In the Soviet Union, a dictator named Joseph Stalin is busy wiping out all who might one day oppose him. His favoured method: a single pistol shot to the back of the head – fully reported in the press, as a warning to all who might consider crossing him in future. Familiar?

Over the next six years, populism and extremism spread across Europe. Hitler, Stalin, Benito Mussolini and Francisco Franco preach hatred and consolidate their power. The term 'propaganda' begins to take on its now familiar meaning and a young political writer, George Orwell, realises that facts are not only being disputed, they are also being invented. News is becoming fake. The populist dictators become commonplace, accepted, respectable. When they ask for national boundaries to be revised and treaties to be abandoned, many see the logic of their case and negotiate with them. And then, when they break their word, their opponents do nothing. *Tick, tick, tick* . . .

By 1936, the first battles of the new age start in Europe – in Spain. The open-air massacres of thousands of innocent people – in town squares and bullfighting rings – begin.

The first cities are terror-bombed. In Guernica, where hundreds are killed, the German perpetrators fabricate fantastic evidence that the Basques destroyed their own city to embarrass the Luftwaffe. The world looks on, horrified, but does little to intervene. *It is just a local war*, the nervous statesmen say. *Not our fight. And anyway, what can we do? Tick, tick, tick . . .*

More camps open. In 1935 Germany begins openly to re-arm. The democracies do nothing . . . In 1938 Germany annexes Austria, claiming to return it to the Fatherland. Nothing . . . Six months later, Hitler demands that the German-speaking regions of Czechoslovakia be ceded to Germany as well. The democracies help him, but at least this time they have qualms. They are slowly waking up . . . Then, in November 1938, the sound of breaking glass heralds the beginning of the end for European Jewry. The time to take preventive action has run out.

We all know what happened after 1939. The big tank battles began. Cities were razed. Concentration camps became extermination camps. All those reasons for not acting earlier suddenly sounded like moral cowardice. Something to regret. Midnight approached . . .

We can discern five stages from the 1920s and '30s that we must not allow to repeat:

1. Sowing the wind – we created the economic conditions that made it difficult to maintain social harmony and political stability.

2. Populism – we allowed those willing to exploit hatred to take power and claim legitimacy.

3. Savagery – animated by culture wars and political intolerance, we saw our world descend into a new era of murder and violence that targeted political opponents, journalists, artists and 'the other'.

4. Preliminary war – we let the populists plan and win early wars when standing up to them might have ended their threat.

5. Consequences – we awoke at last to the reality of massacres and world war.

Is the pattern repeating? In this short book – short because we need to digest its message quickly and respond immediately – I set out to show the uncanny similarities between then and now: our unwillingness to see things until it's too late; our vulnerability to demagogues; the anger of our 'betrayed' electorate; the hate-laden speeches of our populist leaders; their shocking brutality towards opponents; the ugliness of our cultural battles; the spreading poison of racism; the steady disappearance of the concept of the truth; the return of war with its medieval massacres and mass bombing of cities. Ultimately, I want people to grasp just how extraordinary and ugly current events are compared to those of just a couple of decades ago, and how totally inadequate our responses. I want the world to recognise that in many crucial ways, the big failures of the 1920s and '30s are already upon us, and that we have to act now on the lessons of those failures to prevent the greater horror of the 1940s also repeating. I provide no step-by-step programme of action; action must respond to fast-changing events. Instead, I sound an alarm. Because before we can save our world from the savage triumph of the populists, we need to wake from our slumbers and recognise the dangerous reality we now inhabit: a world edging ever closer to repeating 1939.

My story concentrates on the patterns of politics observable in the West, mostly in Russia, Ukraine, the rest of Europe and the United States. But readers will recognise where the lessons of the 1920s and '30 have relevance across the world, where nationalist strongmen with nativist agendas are entrenching their long-term power: in the religious exclusivism of Narendra Modi's right-wing Hindu nationalist Bharatiya Janata Party (BJP); in the aggressive territorial revanchism of Xi Jinping's determination to absorb Taiwan and restore China's past greatness; in Recep Tayyip Erdoğan's authoritarian presidential rule in Turkey; and in Indonesia, where the newly elected former military officer Prabowo Subianto is entering the presidency with a notorious record of human rights abuse. All will be watching to see whether, in such an unpropitious environment, democracies have the resolve to defend their liberal values or surrender them to populist challengers.

So let's observe events as they unfolded, using, where we can, the insights of the people who saw it all going wrong and tried to stop what followed. And let's commence where it all started to go wrong: when the young began to die.

PART I

TRAGEDY

War! I started thinking about it again. It's coming soon, that's certain.

– **George Orwell,** *Coming Up for Air*, **1939**

CHAPTER 1

SOWING THE WIND

Wednesday 12th March 1919, the arrival of Spring. Siegfried Sassoon, captain in the Royal Welch Fusiliers, returned to his rooms in Merton Street Oxford to find a letter on the writing table by the window. His spirits were low. Even opening the cheerful polychromatic curtains given to him by the socialite Ottoline Morrell, revealing the sunny view across Merton College's gardens towards Christ Church Meadows, couldn't brighten him. He had come to Oxford to gain some sort of mental equilibrium after four years of war. Peace had come and like hundreds of millions of people across the world, he needed to 'adjust'. He didn't quite know what he had expected to find in the university town – seriousness maybe, or perhaps a mental peace so that he could put war poetry behind him for good. Instead, he had been vacuumed up into endless socialising, whose gaiety was beginning to anger him. The young were prancing about, lightly touching the ground, as if the past four years had never happened. His brother Hamo, his best friend David Thomas, and his poetic disciple Wilfred Owen – the latter killed pointlessly in the last week of the war – appeared to have died for nothing. Memories of their faces, their peculiar walks, their voices . . . were starting to fade. It was only sixteen weeks since the Armistice had brought the murdering to an end, but the people had already moved on, like onlookers after a cleared up automobile accident. An election had been held and the politicians had already turned the deaths of his beloved friends into revenge and votes, and the makings of another war.

Wearily, he sat at his chair and opened the message. It was on War Office letterhead. He had been officially discharged from service. His army days were over. Here was the final break from the slaughter. A time to start again, and to accept the gay parties without guilt. A time to sing. Instead, an anger filled him. He reached for his pen and writing pad and, in that way he commonly wrote, as if from memory even though the words were wholly new, began to write. It all came flooding back: the fighting at Mametz, the rats, the stench, the corpses decaying in the front line trench, the cold, dirty rain. Then the question that had was now filling every waking and nightmarish thought:

Do you ever stop and ask, 'Is it all going to happen again?'

The Great War would haunt Sassoon for the rest of his life and no matter how hard he tried to get everyone to remember the horrors, and keep remembering them, for many it all soon began to fade. It was all going to happen again, alright – that much seemed certain. Within just four months and one day, humanity had made its first step towards another war. It had started to forget. The second disaster wouldn't be long in coming.

◊

Four and a half years earlier, in early August 1914, the 31-year-old Treasury official John Maynard Keynes watched in despair as his beloved King's College in Cambridge emptied of undergraduates, rushing off to enlist in the newly declared war against Germany. One of them, a patriotic Hungarian named Ferenc Békássy, had decided to return to Hungary to fight for the enemy. Failing to dissuade him but respecting his friend's wishes, Keynes high-mindedly paid his fare for the journey home.

Some eight months later, on 25th April 1915, Keynes fell into a depression. The day prior, he had learned that two young college students he had been fond of had been killed in the early fighting in France. Now, even worse news had arrived: another Kingsman, the famous poet Rupert Brooke, was also dead. 'It is too horrible, a nightmare to be stopt anyhow,' Keynes wrote to his lover, Duncan Grant. 'May no other generation live under the cloud we have to live under.' Three months later, Békássy too was dead. Keynes, always philosophically and intuitively against the war, was beginning to grasp its true human horror.

◊

By the time the war finally ended, on 11th November 1918, Keynes' friends had joined one of the great slaughters of human history. The catastrophe had swallowed up 1.8 million Germans, 1.7 million Russians, 1.4 million French, 1.3 million Austro-Hungarians, three-quarters of a million British, and another 200,000 from the British Empire. The dead were not the only victims. The broken bodies and scarred minds were countless.

Inevitably, Keynes was suffering from a heavy conscience. To the question 'What did *you* do in the war?' he might have answered: 'I did my best to keep it away from my friends and the parts of civilisation I valued.' As a senior adviser to the Treasury, he had begun in 1914 by trying to limit the war's effect on Britain – by arguing that Britain's contribution should be naval and financial, blockading German ports and funding others to do the bulk of the fighting. He wanted Britain to contribute two dozen field divisions, not the seventy Prime Minister Lloyd George later got. If soldiers had to die, Keynes reasoned, best that they were people he didn't know. But Lloyd George won the argument, leading to the slaughters of the Somme, Passchendaele and the Hindenburg Line.

Privately, Keynes had wanted negotiations and a peace compromise, but his day job was to help finance the killing, mainly with American money. 'I work for a government I despise for ends I think criminal,' he wrote to Duncan Grant. David 'Bunny' Garnett, a friend whom Keynes had helped keep out of the fighting, told him he was a 'genie taken incautiously out of King's [College] . . . by savages to serve them faithfully for their savage ends'. You can see Keynes' problem. During the war, even his closest friends had started to disrespect him. But now, with the fighting finally over, he was determined to make amends. He was going to try to stop it all happening again.

◊

In January 1919 Keynes was in France as chief Treasury representative to the British delegation at the Paris Peace Conference. He soon lost heart. The politicians were playing their usual games, courting popularity by trying to make the Germans accept guilt for the war and pay for the damage they had caused, using money they didn't have. To Keynes this was folly, a 'concoction of greed and sentiment, prejudice and deception'. How could mere words on a dictated treaty magically maintain the peace, especially now that the will, and the armies needed to enforce it, had melted away? It was madness. How could the politicians not see that east of France and Belgium, Europe was in the throes of violent revolution and vicious anarchy? Empires, governments, bureaucracies, police forces, ruling classes, legal systems, food distribution and an ordered and peaceful way of life . . . all were dissolving simultaneously.

The newspapers were full of horrors. The revolution in Russia had spread to Germany and Hungary. Bands of angry, demobilised troops roamed the cities and countryside looking for Reds and food, slaughtering their opponents and assassinating their leaders. Children were dying of malnutrition, their parents of tuberculosis, some having lost limbs or their minds. 'In continental Europe,' Keynes wrote, 'the earth heaves and no one but is aware of the rumblings. There it is not just a matter of extravagance or "labour troubles"; but of life and death, of starvation and existence, and of the fearful convulsions of a dying civilisation.' He could feel the rumblings under civilisation's feet. He knew that the vicious, murdering populists were coming.

The only hope was to get the politicians and the people to recognise that the answer lay not in political punishment or the exchange of territories but in restoring finance, trade and prosperity. Keynes had grasped a truth others had yet to see: 'Men will not always die quietly.' Feed them and a return to normalcy was possible.

Keynes resigned from his job at the Treasury, returned to his rooms at Cambridge and, sitting in his favourite armchair, with a board on his lap, poured his anguish into a short book: *The Economic Consequences of the Peace*.

Successfully settling the peace, it argued, required the Allied leaders at Versailles to accept the very thing they couldn't accept: that Germany had to be assisted back to economic greatness. Reparations had to be limited, German war debts guaranteed by all, and its rebuilding financed by bonds backed by American loans. Only then could trade and prosperity return to Europe. If not, there were two stark alternatives for Germany: revolution or reaction. Which would it be?

But the leaders didn't listen. The punitive reparations bill and war guilt clause remained. The wind had been sowed.

CHAPTER 2

POPULISM

Let's go back to 13th November 1919. The Eberlbräu Keller in Munich was a small space compared with the Bürgerbräukeller and the Zirkus Krone, but 130 people could create a decent atmosphere there – which was all a tyro-orator could ask. A new speaker was on his feet. He was representing the German Workers' Party, one of many *völkisch* (populist and racist) organisations that had sprung up on the right of German politics since the end of the war, attracting small memberships of extremists and crackpots.

This speaker had addressed such party meetings only a handful of times, but word had got around that he was a bit of a livewire. His ranting orations had been getting better and better. The secret, he had discovered, was to experiment and find out which messages and lines got the most cheering and applause. If the crowd reacted enthusiastically to any argument or slogan, he would note it down carefully and use it again. A speech packed with lines that reliably elicited wild cheers couldn't fail. In this way, with considerable practice, he had perfected the art of tapping the deep, dark well of resentment and fury that lay just beneath the surface of his audiences – mostly angry men, Stormtroopers maybe, veterans of the artillery barrages, who had faced the tanks and could recall the odour of the gas lurking in the crevices of their blockhouses and dugouts during the big battles and retreats of the year before.

His message tonight was one that never failed to get them going: the Treaty of Versailles, with its reparations and war guilt clauses, forced upon Germany by the 'November criminals' – Marxists and communists whose revolutions and constitutions and foreign ideas had stabbed Germany's unbeaten forces in the back. 'As long as the earth has existed, no people have ever been forced to declare themselves willing to sign such a shameful treaty,' he said. From behind the veil of cigarette smoke and wall of beer glasses came yells in response: 'The work of the Jews!' The speaker took note.

This was the moment to pivot. He let loose against the Reich finance minister, Matthias Erzberger – one of those criminals who negotiated and signed the armistice agreement of 11th November the year before. A Catholic, but the drinkers seemed to hate him all the same. The speaker was certain, he said, 'that the man who had hung such a treaty around our necks would not be in his post for much longer and would not even be a schoolteacher in Buttenhausen'. The implication was ominous, and obvious. Someone ought to kill him.

Amid the cheers, someone yelled out, chillingly: 'He'll get it like Eisner.'

Curious, wasn't it; even when he was attacking a Catholic, the crowd still brought up a Jew – Kurt Eisner, briefly president of Bavaria during the bohemian left-wing revolution of a year before, until a rabid nationalist calmly pulled out a pistol and shot him dead on the street.

At this time, such orators seemed to be on every street corner and on the stage of every beer cellar in Munich. Wild-eyed, racist groups like the Thule Society and militias like the Steel Helmets abounded. But few of their leaders could hold an audience as well as this one, who was simultaneously unafraid, unrestrained and coarse. Later, people would say of this orator that, having heard him speak, they had no choice but to fight and, if necessary, die with him. His name was Adolf Hitler. By then the small party this Hitler spoke for had changed its name to the National Socialist German Workers' Party, popularly known as the Nazis.

It was increasingly obvious to all that Hitler and his followers were creating a murderous political atmosphere, threatening assassinations and pogroms and coups. Walther Rathenau, soon to be foreign minister, and the highest-ranked Jew in the new Weimar government, sensed the danger. Such populists, he warned, were bombarding the ignorant with mistruths and hatred that would divide

Germany beyond repair. Leaders, Rathenau said, had a duty to avoid this behaviour and engage in civilised debate.

Less than two years later, Erzberger was assassinated by hard-right extremists. And nine months after that, Rathenau was as well. In a country awash with guns, as post-war Germany was, first they denounced you a traitor and criminal, then they waited for some extremist or madman acting out of patriotic instinct to shoot you. That was generally how it worked.

◊

Fringe intellectuals are always drawn to anarchic, lawless periods, eager to offer loaded historical explanations for their nation's dramatic collapse, and to prophesy the coming of a new national revival. One such thinker was Arthur Moeller van den Bruck, who in 1923 published a book called *The Third Reich*. According to Moeller van den Bruck, the first two German empires – of Charlemagne and Bismarck – should arise again through a nationalist revolution that would unite the country to restore Germany's medieval glory and make it great once again. A Third Reich . . . it was a useful and messianic political concept no populist could resist. Certainly not Hitler.

◊

The big problem for any nationalist revolutionary, of course, is how to get into power, especially when – as for Hitler in 1922 – your party is only 8000 members strong in a population of 65 million. Fortunately, Benito Mussolini had just shown the way. As historian Mark Jones has pointed out, the Fascist movement decried the Italian capital as a political swamp whose rotten, bribed elite was ruining the country. In response, they plotted to stage a march on Rome, seize power, rebuild a new Italy and recreate the greatness of the Roman Empire.

By the end of October 1922 Mussolini's plan was in place: fascists would seize police and government buildings across Italy and shut down communications and transport. The best fascist fighters, having concentrated themselves in the towns closest to Rome, would then march on the capital and demand Mussolini be handed power, using violence to crush resistance if necessary. If they failed, they would retreat to their strongholds and begin a civil war. The army and police, loyal to King Victor Emmanuel III, could easily have crushed them at this point, but didn't. The king hesitated. The coup succeeded. Mussolini was named prime minister and stayed in power for more than two decades. Half a million Italians died as a result.

A pattern for right-wing populist seizure of power was now established: take the capital, demand power, drain the political swamp, make the nation great again. Hitler looked on enviously and decided to copy it as soon as he could.

◊

As Keynes had predicted, Germany couldn't pay its war reparations. By December 1922 the German government was requesting a pause of two years. The Reparations Commission – created at Versailles to set and oversee Germany's repayments – said no, and on 11th January 1923 French and Belgian troops occupied Germany's industrial heartland, the Ruhr, purportedly to extract payments in coal and timber, but mostly to put pressure on Germany to pay reparations in full. Two days later, the government in Berlin announced a policy of passive resistance. Industrial and agricultural production slowed, unemployment rose from already high levels and the starvation and destitution that had haunted the streets since the middle of the war worsened. Without trade, foreign debts couldn't be paid. Government revenues dried up, but huge sums had to be found to pay wages and pensions and unemployment benefits. There seemed no sensible way out. Raising taxes was rendered politically impossible by populists like Hitler, who claimed the revenue would be used to pay reparations and therefore concede Germany's war guilt. The government began printing money.

The inevitable result was inflation. Or, rather, hyperinflation, on a scale the world had never seen. Money began to lose its value, until it had none at all. In 1914 a US dollar exchanged for 4 German marks. In November 1918, 8 marks. And in December 1923 it exchanged for 4,200,000,000,000 marks. That's 4.2 trillion. A loaf of rye bread alone cost 233 billion marks. Gangs prowled the cities and countryside in search of goods and food. Prostitution was rife. Homicides increased. People lost their houses, their life savings, their minds. And their trust in democracy. How could they not?

At rally after rally, Hitler denounced the policy of passive resistance to the Versailles Treaty as a fraud. By creating chaos and undermining German democracy, the French and Belgians were becoming the would-be dictator's greatest political assets. Germany's real enemies, he screeched, were the elites that lay within: the effete democrats, political and cultural Marxists, artists, homosexuals, Jews and others who had betrayed Germany, accepted its war guilt and condemned it to financial servitude. Now he could hope to take power and eliminate them. His days in tiny venues like the Eberlbräu Keller were behind him. A seething mass of right-wing nationalist parties and paramilitary veterans was slowly coalescing, inexorably drawn to his will. Having drowned Eisner's Bavarian revolution in its own blood four years before, these *völkisch* groups dreamed of eliminating the left-wing elites for good. Hitler had a dream too: to imitate Mussolini, put himself at the head of this movement and march on Berlin to cleanse it of the unpatriotic, criminal filth who dominated its politics, and the Jews who poisoned its blood, then make Germany great again.

◊

On the evening of 8th November 1923, flanked by armed paramilitaries, Hitler appeared suddenly at a political rally organised by rivals in the Bürgerbräukeller, ordered one of his stormtrooper guards to fire a pistol-shot into the ceiling and declared that the national revolution was underway, the Bavarian and Reich governments had been deposed and a provisional government had been created. The following day, he declared, would see either a nationalist government in place or the coup members' own deaths.

As coups went, it was an embarrassment. Hitler's ramshackle armed mob paraded angrily and pointlessly through the streets, alternatively heckled and cheered, trying to drum up public support. In the twelve hours that followed, the madness and unpreparedness of the coup were revealed. The culmination, if that is the right word, was a protest march through the centre of the city. Hitler was in the front row, arm in arm with his fellow rebels. A melee ensued. Shooting broke out, fourteen rebels and four policemen lay dead – including the man with whom Hitler had locked arms in the front row. On such close misses depended the lives of tens of millions of people.

So ended the Beer Hall Putsch – Adolf Hitler's feeble attempt to seize power by violent direct action. He realised that without the police and the army onside, such insurrections were doomed to failure. Next time he would be better prepared.

◊

The Weimar Republic, that brave experiment in modern German statehood that followed Germany's military, economic and political collapse in 1918, had been saved because conservatives decided it was still – marginally – in their interests to defend the constitution. Would democracy get lucky a second time?

◊

Hitler slithered away and hid, nursing a broken arm. Three days later he was arrested and charged with the capital crime of high treason. The state had him in jail. Incontrovertibly guilty of insurrection. Bavaria banned the Nazi Party, as Prussia and other states had already done. Now, surely, he was finished.

◊

Here the story should have ended. The Nazi Party should have been outlawed forever and Hitler should have been executed or given a life sentence that would have kept him out of the way in the crises that followed.

Official justice had been severe after the attempted left-wing uprisings that had convulsed Germany since the war's end. Unofficial justice had been even more severe. In January 1919, following the abortive Spartacist Revolt in Berlin, for example, German communist leaders Rosa Luxemburg and Karl Liebknecht had been arrested by the right-wing Freikorps militias, beaten, shot and their battered bodies dumped. In Munich the next month, Kurt

Eisner had been gunned down in the street. In reality, the law didn't apply equally to the right and the left. Democrats may have been in office nationally, but the police and the judiciary remained in the same old reactionary hands. In the Eisner case, the shooter, a right-wing nationalist named Count Anton von Arco-Valley, had been treated with unusual understanding and leniency. In his summing-up, the judge, an arch-conservative named Georg Neithardt, pointed out that Arco-Valley's actions were motivated by 'ardent love for his people and fatherland'. Arco-Valley was sentenced to death, but the next day the Bavarian government passed a unanimous resolution replacing death with life imprisonment. Judge Georg Neithardt. Remember that name.

The case against Hitler was as straightforward as that against Arco-Valley. He had been caught in the act – openly attempting to overthrow the elected governments of Bavaria and the Reich. Plans seized after the melee spelled out plainly Hitler's intention of installing a new constitution that would put him at the head of the Reich government, place his allies in charge of the army and security forces, send all opponents of the new regime to concentration camps and execute any Jews who refused to comply with severe restrictions on their citizenship. During the putsch itself, four policemen had been killed. Hitler, already on probation, was ineligible for leniency. But he had one advantage that the four dead policemen didn't: the judiciary was on his side. Instead of being tried by federal judges under the Law for the Protection of the Republic, which would have produced a long jail sentence or possibly execution, it was arranged for Hitler to be tried in front of the local Bavarian courts, which were notoriously reactionary and anti-Weimar. And in early 1924, the man appointed as presiding judge for the trial was none other than Georg Neithardt.

Powerless and a loser, a depressed Hitler briefly contemplated suicide. But the prospect of a public trial filled him with joy. It would put him in the spotlight and allow him to demonstrate that he was being persecuted by the elite enemies of the German people for trying to make Germany great again. The judges treated Hitler as a celebrity, permitting him to hold forth for hour after hour, barely interrupting his political speeches, which they allowed to be greeted with public applause. When it was over, they declared him guilty of high treason and gave him a five-year sentence, with possible suspension for good behaviour after just six months. Plus, a fine of 200 gold marks. The lenient sentence was a scandal. Even those in right-wing legal circles found it hard to accept. The coup leader had been made into a hero with an ennobling backstory as a man of action. The legal system had failed to stop him. Adolf Hitler's career was back on track.

◊

Hitler was delivered to cell 70 in Landsberg Prison, a spacious and extremely comfortable castle room – but only after its previous occupant, Eisner's assassin, Arco-Valley, was found another cell. In the luxury of his new surroundings, Hitler began planning for the future. Coups, he had discovered, were risky and chaotic. Next time his takeover would be legal. And its follow-through more thorough. Movements, like leaders, learn.

With at least six months on his hands and nothing else to do but welcome visitors and plan the re-establishment of his shattered party, he relaxed in his armchair and dictated a book about his story and plans to some fellow prisoners. Its title? *Mein Kampf.* No one reading it could be in any doubt about his warlike intentions, his desire to dominate Eastern Europe and his plans for the Jews, Slavs, Marxists and all the other 'traitors'. And yet no one could quite bring themselves to believe he really – *really* – meant it.

Against overwhelming evidence that he would reoffend, the courts freed Hitler in December 1924 and, three months later, un-banned the Nazi Party. The right had let Hitler off. Now he was sharpening his message for a comeback. All the necessary elements of this message were falling into place in the form of well-crafted myths: the stab in the back by the 'November criminals'; the need for a new Reich to restore Germany's greatness; the necessity of finding a national leader with the ability to make it happen; and the extraordinary leadership qualities of Hitler.

◊

The French and Belgians withdrew from the Ruhr. Slowly, a measure of stability and economic growth returned to Germany. Its recovery was financed by American loans through the Dawes Plan. Like the Locarno Treaty, which had returned Germany to the diplomatic mainstream, the Dawes Plan had been negotiated by the brilliant centrist leader Gustav Stresemann as a way of stabilising the currency, ending hyperinflation and allowing Germany to repay at least some of the reparations it owed. Unemployment fell. Prosperity inched upwards. Some semblance of normalcy returned to German society. Political extremism declined. In the May 1928 Reichstag (parliament) elections, the Nazi Party got just 2.6% of the vote and the German Communist Party (KPD) only 10.6% – meaning fewer than one in seven voters supported the extremes. Germany was getting off its knees and standing up. But the American loans that financed this boom meant major debt. Much of it was short-term, waiting to be called in. After a decade of peace, the economic stability Keynes claimed was necessary for political stability had finally arrived. Or so it seemed. But how long could an economy built on paper bonds last?

◊

Hitler, meanwhile, had been eliminating the weaknesses in his Nazi Party machine. Most importantly, he found a manager who could organise an effective election campaign. Someone who could market him and his party as the wave of the future: a pseudo-intellectual with big and dangerous ideas about national and cultural revival. Someone looking for a leader like Adolf Hitler. His name was Joseph Goebbels.

In addition to providing tight organisation, Goebbels mixed Hitler's ranting ideas into a strong, forward-looking vision and appealing, digestible messages whose effectiveness was reinforced by the latest campaigning techniques: flying Hitler from rally to rally, the use of radio, films, songs, demonstrations, parades and more. Having a profound understanding of the aesthetics of power, Goebbels choreographed Hitler's rallies into ever more spectacular shows able to capture the public imagination. His aim was not just to gain the support of the majority but to bring about a spiritual mobilisation of German society.

◊

In England in 1936, George Orwell took an interest in fascist rallies, seeing how whenever the image of General Franco appeared in cinema newsreels, ecstatic Spaniards stood and raised their arms in salute while young men chanted, *Viva la muerte!* ('Long live death!') over and over again. He also attended a British Union of Fascists rally to see its leader, Sir Oswald Mosley, and heard the crowds of working men chant, 'Mosley! Mosley! Mosley!' as the obviously insincere multimillionaire businessman, who shared nothing of the lives of his followers, addressed them. How easy it seemed, Orwell thought, for such men to bamboozle everyday people with their bigoted nonsense. He noticed how their chanting resembled the bleating of sheep.

◊

Just as the Nazi machine was becoming more potent, the Weimar Republic found itself hampered by another problem. In late 1929 its best political statesman, Stresemann, died of multiple strokes, aged just fifty-one. Denied his moderating influence, the centrist 'Grand Coalition' – comprising the Social Democratic Party (SPD), the Catholic Centre Party, the liberal German Democratic Party (DDP) and the centre-right German People's Party (DVP) – threw away government over a trivial dispute about who should pay for unemployment insurance. In the long and proud history of German social-democratic and liberal politics, this was perhaps the most irresolute, unforgivable, short-sighted moment of them all.

A new government had to be formed. The parties of progress had dealt themselves out of the running. Now it was the conservatives' and reactionaries' turn to decide affairs. And in the wings, agitating, was the freed Adolf Hitler and his legal Nazi Party.

◊

Helping Hitler was the press, especially the media empire of Alfred Hugenberg, former chairman of the Krupp steelworks, which had profited heavily from armaments sales in the First World War. Hugenberg's goal was to overturn the Weimar constitution and replace it with a reactionary regime headed by himself. Media barons are sometimes known to behave like politicians, but Hugenberg was an actual politician – the chairman from 1928 of the increasingly reactionary German National People's Party (DNVP). His political power was such that he was sometimes called the 'uncrowned king' of Germany. Needing a working-class base to fulfil his leadership dreams, Hugenberg sought an alliance with the Nazis, and used his newspapers to propel them from the fringe to the mainstream, giving them much-needed money, media coverage and legitimacy. Hitler, still a relatively minor political player, was now regularly on the front pages of the mass-circulation right-wing newspapers. In today's terms, his 'recognition factor' received a major boost.

The Hugenberg media empire was populist, edgy, loud and unashamedly grubby. Impartiality, balance, the truth and other journalistic values were regarded as out of date. The proprietor intervened constantly in editorial decisions to sow division, polarisation, distrust, doubt, hatred and a sense of crisis – a strategy he called 'catastrophe politics'. Slowly but surely, his media empire's lies and half-truths spread the feeling that the nation was descending into chaos. And alongside all this, his newspapers and film studios waged a vigorous and violent culture war to direct the hatred of the working class away from capitalists like himself and towards artists, professors and elites of all kinds – including Jews, naturally. Unfortunately for Hugenberg, the beneficiary of all this was not himself but the man his newspapers had helped transform from a comparative nobody into a dangerous somebody. A somebody who would recognise no master: Adolf Hitler.

◊

On 24th October 1929, Wall Street crashed, and those American loans were called in. The economic catastrophe arrived. Unemployment was unleashed. Weeks before the crash, official unemployment in Germany had been 1.3 million; by late 1930 it was at 5 million; by 1932 it was at 6 million; and the official statistics far understated the real numbers. Historians of Nazi Germany have described over and again how the sudden onset of the Great Depression destroyed what remained of the always tenuous popular legitimacy of the Weimar Republic. Coming on top of wartime starvation and chronic postwar economic hardships, it convinced millions that democracy could provide no answer to their urgent needs. A feeling of political abandonment and betrayal overwhelmed reason and heightened the demand for a strong man to come in and restore Germany's former glory. In a state of emotional despair, power would be given to those whose extremism had previously made their rule utterly unthinkable.

All dictators seem to want a return to past greatness.

At the elections of September 1930, the Nazi vote increased sevenfold to 18.3%. The political classes were shocked, uncomprehending. They thought the angry, starving working class would flock to the SPD and KPD. How could these populist extremists – amateurs who didn't follow the rules of the political game – be so successful? It didn't make sense. In July 1932, the Nazi vote more than doubled again, to 37.4%. Overwhelmed by the cataclysm of the Depression, which was exacerbated (as Keynes had predicted) by the tone-deaf deflationary, dole-cutting policies of the reactionary Chancellor Heinrich Brüning, people sought revenge. They looked for a leader and party with a simple emotional story and political energy to burn. Ready, willing and free to fill this vacuum was Adolf Hitler, with his vision of punishing the guilty elites and making Germany great again. As two of the leading historians of Nazi Germany, Richard J. Evans and Ian Kershaw, have summed it up, the Nazi pitch to the electorate was less an orthodox political platform than a rhetorical promise of national redemption to overcome the pervasive sense of political, economic and psychological collapse that had descended upon the country. It was a vision of Germany reborn, united, working cohesively through racial unity. Compared to the cautious greyness of the mainstream alternatives, it seemed novel, youthful, energetic and extremely electorally potent.

Yes, Germany would become great again.

◊

At this moment fate tried to give democracy one last chance to reject the populist surge and survive: the economic crisis passed its peak and living conditions began to improve. At the election of November 1932, the Nazis lost 2 million votes and thirty-four seats in the Reichstag, plunging to less than one-third – 31.1% – of the vote. Hitler was humiliated by a series of political misjudgements, which the opposition newspapers reported with glee. The Nazis were despondent; their continuing rise depended on crisis and chaos, and it seemed they had missed their moment. Their members began to lose faith. The party's ranks fell precipitously; its finances were depleted; splits emerged within its branches and violent fighting broke out between factions in its paramilitary wing, the SA (also known as the Stormtroopers or Brownshirts). Worst of all, an alternative and more moderate leader, Gregor Strasser, tentatively challenged Hitler for control and flirted with entering the Reich cabinet. It seemed the Nazis were falling to pieces. Hitler didn't help matters by seemingly losing the plot. His tactical moderation to fool the voters gave way to semi-deranged ranting about liberals, communists, Marxists, Jews and his own frustrated destiny. It was all or nothing, and it looked like nothing would be the result.

If democracy could hold things together for just six more months before the calling of another election, Hitler's forward march would likely be halted.

At this dramatic point in world history, a group of disgruntled conservatives made a fatal error. In the middle of 1932, Brüning's government had been replaced by one led by Franz von Papen. This lasted until December, and then came an administration led by the congenital plotter General Kurt von Schleicher. Papen intensely disliked Schleicher – a past friend who had betrayed him – and wanted revenge. He and the media baron Hugenberg devised a plan: give the chancellorship instead to Hitler, tame him by burdening him with the responsibilities of power, and eventually take power themselves. According to the plan, the SA would be employed to eliminate the communists, before themselves being eliminated by the army. In this way, Papen's and Hugenberg's conservative allies – the bankers, industrialists and aristocratic big landowners – believed they could co-opt Hitler's lower-class support base, smash the communists, the SPD and the centrist liberals, and return Germany to the rule of a conservative and authoritarian elite that would restore the army to its former glory and cut taxes and regulations for big business. Hitler would get the chancellorship, but only if he agreed to have a non-Nazi majority in his cabinet, Papen as his vice-chancellor and Hugenberg running the economy. Hitler would be the conservative establishment's puppet. The man, after all, was an unsophisticated embarrassment, and his followers the scum of society; aristocrats and generals like Papen and his friends like Hugenberg could control and direct him as they chose. The ingénue would shrink and be overwhelmed.

All they needed was a pliant, right-wing head of state

willing to appoint him. And such a man was already in place – one of the military men who had led Germany to destruction in the great war: Field Marshal Paul von Hindenburg.

To cynical mainstream politicians, the idea of enlisting the Nazis seemed sensible enough: their popular vote would be harnessed and swallowed up; and once in government, Hitler would be forced to face reality, listen to the bankers and the bureaucrats from Treasury, heed the criticisms of the editorial writers, drop his extremism, move back towards the centre just enough to become compliant and govern the way everyone else did. Hugenberg confidently boasted they would 'box Hitler in'. 'In two months, we'll have pushed Hitler so far into a corner so tight he'll squeak,' predicted Papen.

◊

There were only three Nazis in the cabinet Papen had handed Hitler. But what need did he have of a cabinet? Economics didn't interest him. Neither did the law. Nor public administration generally. But he made sure he controlled the police and the streets. He made Wilhelm Frick interior minister and Hermann Göring acting Prussian minister of the interior – which gave the Nazi Party control of the national and Prussian state police. Unhindered by the law, the Brownshirts immediately let loose a reign of terror, beating and murdering communists, then social democrats, as they pleased. The leftists were sacked from their public service jobs. Their newspapers were banned. Their political offices, trade union headquarters and family homes were raided and vandalised. They were arrested and sent to special camps being hastily set up. Later, the Catholic Centre Party members would follow.

One of the first actions of the incoming cabinet was to dissolve the Reichstag and call new elections. Hitler made it clear that the election would be the last and, regardless of the result, he would not resign. Anyway, he had no intention of making the election free and fair.

On 27th February, a lonely Dutch anarchist named Marinus van der Lubbe set fire to the Reichstag building. Watching the flames, Hitler said: 'There will be no more mercy now; anyone who stands in our way will be butchered.' False news was spread of a planned communist uprising. An emergency decree was drawn up, taking away all individual freedoms and placing all power to act against disruptors of public order in the hands of the cabinet, not the president. The arrest lists had already been prepared. The Marxists were rounded up. Within two weeks, 10,000 communists were in jail. To help house them, a camp was opened on the outskirts of Munich in a town named Dachau. Other camps followed. By the end of 1933, more than 130,000 communists had been arrested and 2500 murdered.

With all this vigorous action against terrorists forming the backdrop of the election campaign, the Nazis increased their vote share to 43.9%. They never actually gained an electoral majority anywhere, but experience had taught them to have a majority where it counted: in the police, on the judicial benches, on the streets and in the military.

◊

Hitler allowed the newly elected Reichstag to sit for one day: 23rd March 1933. Its job was to pass the *Enabling Act*, which effectively put all legislative authority in his hands and abolished German democracy and individual liberty.

On the square in front of the Reichstag that day, Hitler had assembled a wild squad of angry Nazi members and SA militiamen, who chanted and jostled and abused the deputies as they entered, trying to intuit the leader's wishes. The elected communist deputies were absent; those not already dead were in hiding or in jail; certainly none was foolish enough to show up. The SPD deputies courageously did show up, even though some of their comrades had already been murdered. Once inside the chamber, they were confronted by the sight of a huge swastika hanging from the ceiling and Brownshirts lining the walls and blocking the exits. It had come to this: the violent militias, now commonplace on the streets, had made it inside the legislature itself, to make the people's will clear. Many SPD deputies expected to be beaten up and killed.

Hitler, no longer the apprentice of early beer-cellar

days, now wearing Brownshirt uniform, made a two-and-a-half-hour speech about the 'national decay caused by the mistaken teachings of Marxism' and the need to 'morally cleanse the body of the people', before mouthing vague promises to make agriculture once again profitable for farmers, protect the middle classes from competition and give workers back their spending power. To the Social Democrats, pressured to pass the *Enabling Act*, he thundered: 'Now, gentlemen, you may decide whether it's to be war or peace.'

Afterwards, the SPD chairman Otto Wells made a stirring appeal. 'You can take away our liberty, and our lives,' he said, 'but not our honour,' to which the Nazi delegates replied with mocking laughter. Hitler responded as a bully in a playground might, calling them 'whiny and unfit for the coming age'. Only the SPD delegates opposed the law – showing political clarity that had maybe come too late. The liberal and moderate conservative parties that had once proudly supported German constitutionalism, freedom and individual rights voted for the *Enabling Act* and effectively abolished themselves.

◊

Among the observers of Hitler's takeover in the late winter and early spring of 1933 was the English poet and novelist Christopher Isherwood, who used the experience as material for his novel *Goodbye to Berlin*. One moment it seemed his communist friends were in charge of the streets (at least in Berlin), taunting and humiliating the ridiculous-looking Brownshirts. But suddenly, everything changed. Isherwood was soon reporting in his diary that Schleicher had resigned and Hitler had formed a cabinet with Hugenberg. No one, he wrote, thought it could last more than a few weeks.

More than forty years later, Isherwood would admit that he himself was one of those who thought Hitler's rule couldn't last. His appointment as chancellor, he wrote, was a lucky break because it would expose his obvious inability to cope with the economic disaster he had inherited, highlight his utter windbaggery, force his rapid resignation, and discredit the Nazis forever.

Many took refuge in this flimsy optimism, even those who had the most to lose, including some of Isherwood's politically less astute homosexual friends, whose defiant behaviour made them easily identifiable and vulnerable. The prudent, he reported, were terrified and cautious, while the less astute pranced around the city praising the sexiness of the stormtrooper uniforms. Such self-delusion must have some sort of explanation – apart, of course, from naivety and political ignorance (to which Isherwood freely confessed). It came from the idea that the Nazis were so unconventional in their approach to politics that they couldn't possibly succeed. The rules of the political game – which held that political outcomes were limited by an Overton window of conventional opinion – would reassert themselves soon enough and the Nazis' pathetic attempt to subvert political reality would soon be exposed as an aberration. Blink during their rule, and you might miss it. But the Nazis soon demonstrated that the Overton window was a dangerous fallacy that bred complacency.

◊

By May 1933 Isherwood's friends had lost their optimistic illusion that once Hitler got into power, he would renounce his extremism and govern pragmatically. On the 6th, Berlin's *Institut für Sexualwissenschaft*, which advocated for what we would today call LGBTQ+ rights, and which Isherwood frequented, was raided by Nazi students and smashed up. A few days later, Isherwood watched on as the institute's books and papers were burned in the Opernplatz public square, along with a bust of the institute's founder, Magnus Hirschfeld – a Jew. The books of Bertolt Brecht, Ernest Hemingway, Thomas and Heinrich Mann, Stefan Zweig and many more 'anti-German' authors went up in flames along with them. The Nazi propaganda chief, Goebbels, was there to speak and praise the young activists for their foresight. The scene was repeated across nearly three dozen German university towns. Isherwood, who was present at the burning, shouted 'shame', but not so loudly.

◊

The cabarets, gay bars and left-wing cafés where Isherwood spent his time quickly became too dangerous to visit. One by one, his friends were beaten up and dragged away. The realists recognised that it was time to flee this unrecognisable Germany, now run by intolerant thugs. Isherwood, too, saw that he should return home to England, where the law still meant something. On his last day in Berlin, he took a walk in the spring sunshine. Hitler, he recorded, was now master of the city and dozens of his friends were in prison, possibly dead. It had taken no time at all for the horror to happen.

◊

After just five months of Hitler's rule – on 27th June 1933 – the great media puppet master Hugenberg was forced out of Hitler's cabinet, his portfolios taken by Nazis, and his party, the DNVP, dissolved. Hugenberg's final instruction to his party executive was to go home and crawl into their closets or hide in the woods. Hitler then brought Rudolf Hess and others into the cabinet, giving it a Nazi majority. Joseph Goebbels got Hugenberg's job and official government flat. A week after that, the Catholic Centre Party, which had acquiesced in Hitler's takeover by voting for the enabling bill, was also dissolved. By July, all parties other than the Nazi Party were outlawed, and forming a new party meant the death penalty.

By the end of 1933, the churches had been silenced, the army had been brought under control, and the non-Nazi conservative nationalist members of the cabinet who had put Hitler in power and thought they could control him had been swatted aside. In December, Hugenberg's media empire was swallowed up by the propaganda ministry and the state news agency, proving that media barons serve populists at their own risk. It seemed Hugenberg now needed Hitler more than Hitler needed Hugenberg. Papen survived within the government a year longer, before being shunted off to the diplomatic corps.

And in the middle of the next year, on the Night of the Long Knives, Hitler wiped out everyone on the right who had opposed his rule or could be considered a threat: moderate Nazis like Gregor Strasser, who had refused to do what Hitler told them; old conservative politicians like Gustav Ritter von Kahr, who had opposed Hitler in 1923; reactionary Prussian politician-generals like Kurt von Schleicher, who had opposed him in 1933; and even the violent leader of the Brownshirts, Ernst Röhm, whose militia had made it possible for Hitler to prevail. No one was safe.

Having refused to take Hitler's populist threat seriously and having handed him power thinking they could control him, the German right-wing establishment, including its dominant right-wing media empire, was destroyed, its leaders irrelevant or dead. As the writer Sebastian Haffner later put it, non-Nazis were completely overwhelmed, suffering severe shock from their smashing and unexpected defeat. All of their defences had been overcome and organised resistance suddenly seemed hopeless.

No one had taken seriously the prospect that Hitler's populist juggernaut could actually take power. Certainly not back in 1923, after his failed coup. But here he was, doing exactly what he said he would do: establishing a dictatorship. Even then, many thought he didn't really mean it. And it had all taken less than eighteen months.

The wealthy and powerful, looking to harness the power of the angry *little* people, had helped put Hitler in the Reich chancellery, but he was determined to rule without them. This should have been obvious to all from the start, and now it was too late for hindsight and regrets. That's what happens when you cut cards with the devil.

Then there was the matter of the Jews. Populism always seems to have something in surprise for them. Their reckoning was to come.

◊

In a late scene in *Cabaret*, the 1972 movie adaptation of Isherwood's *Goodbye to Berlin*, the lead character, Brian Roberts, is shown relaxing in a pleasant beer garden on a sunny afternoon. He is with the aristocratic, politically naive industrialist Max von Heune when members of the Hitler Youth start singing the mock Nazi anthem 'Tomorrow Belongs to Me', with its forebodings of conflict and promise of deliverance for the glorious Fatherland. Nazi salutes thrust to the sky as the young voices are gradually joined by all present, except for Brian, Max and one old man, a worker, whom one assumes to be a communist or social democrat and maybe a veteran of the trenches, who knows what horrors will follow. As they are leaving, Brian, a smile on his face, turns to Max and asks him whether he still thinks he can control this Hitler and his Nazi rabble.

CHAPTER 3

SAVAGERY

It is hard to believe, but even as late as 1932, Joseph Stalin, general secretary of the Communist Party of the Soviet Union, faced serious opposition. Old Bolshevik and Central Committee member Martemyan Ryutin, appalled at the famine caused by Stalin's collectivisation drive, wrote and distributed a 200-page denunciation of the tyrannical leader, calling for his overthrow. For such bravery, he was arrested, tried and imprisoned – and five years later rearrested, retried and shot.

If opposition to Stalin was risky, rivalry was suicidal. This was especially so when the rival had recently won more votes for election to the Central Committee than Stalin and had a powerbase Stalin couldn't control. Such a man was Sergei Kirov, First Secretary of the Communist Party in Leningrad. In Stalin's Russia, such a person always died suddenly, based on orders that could never be proven to have come from the top.

On 1st December 1934, while walking through the corridors of the party headquarters in Leningrad, Kirov's bodyguard dropped back and an unemployed former party member, Leonid Nikolaev, appeared, pulled out a Nagant revolver and shot Kirov in the back of the neck – the signature execution method of the NKVD (the People's Commissariat for Internal Affairs, as the secret police were called). Stalin rushed from Moscow to the scene of the crime to state that the bullet had been fired not at one man but at the revolution itself, and to announce emergency anti-terrorism laws allowing the rapid trial and execution of anyone accused of terrorism. Kirov's bodyguard died soon after, unluckily falling off an NKVD truck on his way to interrogation. The shooter was quickly tried and killed under the new laws. The NKVD men who had handled the shooter were swept up, sent to posts in the provinces, then shot three years later.

This was just the beginning of the Terror – or, at least, of the urban terror; the countryside had already been sieved of potential enemies. In Leningrad, anyone not an Old Bolshevik with proletarian credentials became suspect. In fact, just about everyone became suspect, including intellectuals and artists – but we'll come back to them. The late-night knocks on the door began. People prepacked bags with lots of warm underwear, ready for their new Gulag home in the Arctic Circle. Others, less strong, or maybe stronger, committed suicide. Sought-after apartments suddenly became vacant. This went on for two years, then the consequences of Kirov's death really hit home. Things got even worse.

◊

Let's assume the NKVD was involved in Kirov's death, as many claim. Its head in 1934 was Genrikh Yagoda. Two years later Stalin disposed of Yagoda, replaced him with his friend Nikolai Yezhov and got Yezhov to fit up two other Old Bolshevik rivals of Stalin's – Grigory Zinoviev and Lev Kamenev – for Kirov's assassination. They painted it as part of a plot masterminded by that other rival, Leon Trotsky, to destroy the revolution. Let's call this Moscow Show Trial Number 1.

As their name suggests, these Moscow show trials were carried out in the spotlight of the world's media to convey to any remaining unobservant soul that opposing Stalin meant death. Stalin, in fact, had the trials carefully scripted, like Hollywood movies, to produce the required effect, and personally amended the transcripts of the traitors' confessions afterwards. Occasionally, the accused 'forgot' their lines.

Two more big show trials followed: Moscow Show Trial Number 2, in which the Old Bolsheviks Georgy Pyatakov and Karl Radek were disposed of, and Moscow Show Trial Number 3, in which Nikolai Bukharin and Alexei Rykov were farewelled into their graves.

Those sentenced to death rather than a gulag were taken to a cellar in Moscow's Lubyanka Prison, specially constructed with a sloping floor and drainage outlet, where they were shot in the back of the head with a Nagant revolver. The resulting blood, brain and skull fragments were hosed down the drain and into the sewerage system. Others, like Rykov, were imprisoned in an Arctic penal colony for long enough to be forgotten, then beaten to death out of the spotlight. Ordinary folk were simply rounded up and shot without the need for a show trial. Given the enormous numbers involved, show trials for all would have been impracticable.

◊

Back in England, George Orwell, convalescing in a tuberculosis sanatorium after dodging fascist and communist bullets in Spain, read about these trials in *The Times* and was astonished. What was going on in communist Russia didn't seem very different from what was going on in Nazi Germany, he thought.

◊

Political rivals to Stalin obviously couldn't live long. What about artists?

Let's start with the writers. Or, more precisely, the poets – the revolution's equivalents of today's pop stars.

As always in revolutions, poets were initially tolerated, even feted. Alexander Blok, the great symbolist poet of pre-revolutionary Russia, hailed for his messianic 1918 poem

'The Twelve', which likened a group of Red Guards to the Christian Apostles, fell out of favour by 1921 and was denied permission to travel abroad to seek medical help. Not even the pleas of the favoured Maxim Gorky could get the regime to relent. Blok died, disillusioned, in August of that year. Three weeks later, the more conservative poet Nikolai Gumilev was arrested and shot by the Cheka – the forerunner to the NKVD – after being implicated in an invented conspiracy. Another poet initially celebrated by the regime, Sergei Yesenin, died by suicide in December 1925. The futurist poet Vladimir Mayakovsky lasted a bit longer, but shot himself in April 1930 after being denounced for satirising the Soviet bureaucracy and economic policies. (Or he was murdered. It wasn't quite clear, as usual. Ten days later, the investigating officer was killed.)

The next poet to suffer was an Acmeist named Osip Mandelstam. In the year of Kirov's assassination, the celebrated Mandelstam, outraged by the collectivisation policy, had recited to colleagues a poetic attack on Stalin, 'The Stalin Epigram', which unwisely compared the leader to a cockroach. Word of this spread, until someone – maybe out of jealousy, maybe to save themselves – told the authorities. Arrested, roughly interrogated, exiled and rehabilitated, he was scooped up again three years later and died of typhus in transit to the Arctic Circle in the winter of 1938, just as the Terror was coming to an end. It was reported that, following his final interrogation, he appeared at times to be quite insane. His wife, Nadezhda

Mandelstam, denied work rights, a ration card and a place to live, was forced to live peripatetically, relying on the generosity of fearful friends. She somehow managed to survive until the thaw of the 1950s to write one of the great accounts of the destruction of the Soviet intelligentsia.

Prophetically, Osip Mandelstam had once written: 'Only in Russia is poetry respected – it gets people killed.' He was partly right – prose could get you killed too. This included, almost unbelievably, the most 'Bolshevik' Russian prose writer of the era: Maxim Gorky. Gorky, a friend of Lenin and therefore regarded as untouchable, died supposedly of pneumonia while under house arrest in Leningrad. (Many argue he was poisoned by the NKVD.) If they could hound Maxim Gorky to his death, no artist was safe. That, at least, was the general idea. Populists and revolutionaries can never abide artists for long, at least not while they are alive and capable of writing against the regime. After they die, though, they become useful again. They are rehabilitated, their works are plundered for orthodox messages, and they are turned into deities. The schoolchildren who win prizes for reciting their best verses are never taught about the writers' time as dissidents.

◊

What chance of survival, then, had composers and theatre directors? But before we come to them, we have to consider another group of Russians who also couldn't be allowed to live: army generals, because in Stalin's Russia, artists and generals become strangely enmeshed.

◊

Mikhail Tukhachevsky, marshal of the Soviet Union, winner of the civil war, commander of the Red Army in Ukraine and Poland, the most brilliant and original military thinker in the USSR, champion of the tank and so much more, was also, apparently, a fascist fifth columnist and agent of Nazi Germany. So, one day in May 1937, he was arrested, along with seven other generals, and driven to Lubyanka in a prison van. When, some days later, Tukhachevsky and his companions appeared in court (let's call this Moscow Show Trial Number 4) to confess that they were part of Trotsky's grand conspiracy to betray the Soviet state and restore capitalism, the military judges noticed that, beneath the marshal's facial bruises and cuts, his nose was broken. It was said that NKVD head Yezhov himself had supervised the beating. Hearing the accusations read to him in court, Tukhachevsky was heard to say: 'I feel I'm dreaming.' The judges declared him guilty, of course. The bullet to the back of the head came shortly after midnight. Over the years, the blood splattered across his signed confession reacted chemically with the paper and turned brown, as it remains today.

Almost the entire military leadership followed Tukhachevsky to the basement of the Lubyanka. Altogether, 544 of the 767 members of the High Command were shot, died in prison or by suicide. Another fifty-nine survived jail. And when men like Tukhachevsky fell, so did their friends.

◊

One such unfortunate man was the famous composer, Dmitri Shostakovich.

Poets and writers at least produce words, which have definable meanings. A poem like Mandelstam's, aimed at Stalin, had obvious counter-revolutionary intent. How, though, could music without lyrics possibly be subversive? In a world ruled by populists, culture is never harmless, and artists, especially courageous and talented artists, can always be relabelled as elitist enemies of the people when it suits the leader. Sometime after Stalin made clear his dislike of Shostakovich's music in 1936, a notice appeared in the official Communist Party newspaper, *Pravda*, telling its readers that that day a concert was to be given by the enemy of the people, Shostakovich.

Naturally Shostakovich sought help from a high-up friend, someone he had often played music with: Marshal Tukhachevsky. So when Tukhachevsky fell, Dimitri Shostakovich found himself a guest of the NKVD. His interrogator wanted to know more about his association with his powerful (now dead) patron. 'Come back on Monday morning, comrade, when we will continue our little discussion.' Over the weekend, Shostakovich packed his case, which sat ready by the door of his apartment on Kirovsky Prospect, worked on some compositions to distract himself from his fears, and said farewell to his wife, baby and friends. It was obviously the end. As ordered, three days later he reported to his interrogator. But Comrade Interrogator wasn't there; he too had been denounced and arrested. In this mad, random way, the case of Dmitri Shostakovich, potential counter-revolutionary, fascist and Gulag labourer, was lost in the swirl of chaos and fear and misplaced files that gripped the NKVD, the Red Army and everyone else in the Soviet Union. He lived on . . .

Other musicians weren't as fortunate. Anyone in any way futuristic, avant-garde or maybe just talented was threatened. Shostakovich's close friend, the famed experimental theatre director Vsevolod Meyerhold, was next. In 1936 his works were denounced as alien to the Soviet people and his theatre was closed. Bravely, but probably unwisely, in 1939 he denounced the Soviet Union's official anti-formalist art policy. He was arrested three days later, savagely tortured in the basement of the Lubyanka and shot in the usual way. While this was happening, his apartment was broken into and his wife was stabbed to death. Finally, wives were being murdered too. Composer of factory-machine music Alexander Mosolov – gulag. Futurist composer Gavriil Popov – banned. Shostakovich's lyrical collaborator Boris Kornilov – shot.

As in Germany at that time, anyone or anything associated with high art was suspect. Culture was a battleground. The creative were forced into self-censorship or the production of crude propaganda. Books were restricted and disappeared from libraries. Populism thrives on culture wars.

◊

Some dissidents were lucky enough to be exiled. Safely outside the borders of the Soviet Union, they could breathe a little easier, knowing they wouldn't be ending up like poor old Kirov, Bukharin, Kamenev, Zinoviev, Radek and Tukhachevsky. No show trials and bullets to the back of the head for them. Or so they thought.

Even back in the 1930s, terror had to be global in order to be effective. How could dictators scare people into political silence when they could simply move their writing and organising overseas, as Karl Marx had after he moved to London in 1850?

Leon Trotsky did this too. Trotsky – avowed leader of the 1905 revolution, chairman of the Petrograd Soviet in 1917, negotiator of the Treaty of Brest-Litovsk in 1918, commander of the Red Army during the civil war – was the highest-profile leader of the opposition inside the revolutionary state, a glamorous, globally recognised dissident. From Turkey, France, Norway and finally Mexico, he penned book after book, outlining the betrayal of communism under Stalin, urging the few remaining members of the left opposition in the Soviet Union to stand firm against the tyranny and calling for a new international workers' uprising to overthrow the betrayed revolution. He even created the Fourth International organisation to lead this new global proletarian revolt. But Trotsky and the others were wrong. Even outside the borders of the Soviet Union, people like him could not be allowed to live.

In August 1936, Trotsky, exiled since 1928, hounded by Stalin's diplomacy, got his show trial and death sentence *in absentia*. The assassins slipped straight onto his tail. Death became his shadow. They first tried to kill him in March 1939 but failed miserably. The NKVD set up a special commission to do the job properly, sneaking foreign agents into Mexico, where he was living in a high-profile arrangement with the celebrity artists Diego Rivera and Frida Kahlo. The agents tried and failed again in May 1940, leading Trotsky to publish an article telling the world that Stalin was trying to kill him. Still the dictator didn't care . . . all publicity being good publicity.

In August the assassins succeeded. An agent, Rámon Mercader, inveigled his way into Trotsky's life and smashed an ice axe into his skull. As the communist song gruesomely put it: 'Leon Trotsky's got an ice-pick in his head, and he ain't gunna split no more.' Mercader spent twenty years in a Mexican jail for his efforts. His mother was presented with the Order of Lenin on his behalf. The following September, as Hitler's armies drove into Russia, Trotsky's sister, Olga Kameneva, was disposed of by the NKVD in a forest massacre near Orel. (Yes, they had started killing sisters too). No one who ever stood up to the dictator was allowed to live. Absolutely no one. The terror was total. Some 300,000 people passed by Trotsky's casket over five days in Mexico City. *Good*, Stalin thought. *More publicity you can't buy.*

◊

Altogether, during the Terror 700,000 Soviet citizens were executed. Another 389,000 were added to the already crowded gulags, taking the camp population at that time to 1 million. Of the 139 members of the Central Committee at the 1934 Party Congress, ninety-eight were shot. (Some sources say 102). Around 50,000 party members, state officials and Red Army officers were liquidated. The left-wing populist revolution of 1917 had rapidly descended into murderous dictatorship. No one was free. It was inconceivable that Russians could ever allow this to happen again.

CHAPTER 4

PRELIMINARY WAR

On 18th July 1936 the world woke up to discover that military conflict had returned to Europe. The previous day, reactionary Spanish officers who would eventually come under the leadership of General Francisco Franco attempted to seize power across major Spanish cities in a lightning coup.

It was meant to be over in a matter of days. The coup leaders, or 'Nationalists' – a mix of modern fascists, aristocrats and reactionary Catholics, expected little resistance. But the Spanish Republic fought back. A collection of army units loyal to the Republic and hastily thrown-together anarchist and socialist militias repulsed the takeover. Madrid, Barcelona, Valencia and other population centres held firm. A major civil war began. The people of the democratic world rallied to the Republican cause. Idealistic volunteers, mostly from the left, made their way to Madrid and Barcelona to fight. Famous writers, journalists and

Hollywood celebrities lent support to what they described as the struggle to halt the spread of fascism. The Spanish Republic gained many supporters, but what it mostly needed was arms.

On 19th July, head of France's newly elected Popular Front government Léon Blum received a telegram from Spanish prime minister José Giral asking for bombers, guns and ammunition to defend the Republic. Blum's first instinct was to agree. But within days he wavered. The right-wing press had launched a ferocious campaign against French arms sales. British foreign secretary Anthony Eden, influenced by right-wing Spanish diplomats, convinced Blum that the two sides were so evenly matched that providing arms to any side would only prolong the war. On 25th July Blum's cabinet banned arms sales to the Republicans. And on 2nd August Blum's government proposed a policy of non-intervention, in which the governments of France, Britain, Germany and Italy would agree to ban arms sales to either side. So eager was Eden to prevent arms sales that he announced the Royal Navy would enforce an arms blockade of its own until the diplomats of the four nations could agree.

Franco, on the other hand, got everything he wanted from the European fascist powers. Hitler immediately supplied German air force (Luftwaffe) Junkers Ju 52 transport aircraft to ferry units of Franco's Spanish Army of Africa across the Mediterranean, German pocket battleships kept the Spanish Republican Navy from intervening and plentiful weapons and munitions were supplied. The first shipment reached Spain on 1st August, including Panzer 1 tanks and 20mm and 88mm anti-aircraft guns. By November the Luftwaffe itself, in the guise of the Condor Legion, arrived to give Franco aerial superiority. As the war progressed, Hitler would send yet more of the experimental weapons that he would later employ against Poland, the Low Countries, France and Britain: the Stuka dive bomber, the Messerschmitt Me 109 fighter, the Heinkel He 111 and Dornier Do 17 bombers.

Not content to deny arms to the Republicans, the British and French had created a diplomatic front that would allow Nazi Germany and Fascist Italy to arm Franco to the teeth and test the weapons and tactics that would bring the Allies disaster in 1940. The American ambassador to Spain, Claude Bowers, later described the Non-intervention Committee as the most cynical and lamentably dishonest group known to history.

Within three weeks of the civil war starting, Europe's democracies – timid, fearful of provoking Hitler into a war they felt unprepared to fight and afraid of upsetting the right-wing press – had taken the first step towards ensuring that the fascists would win.

But what about America? What would it do? The United States remained staunchly isolationist. Congress had rejected membership of the League of Nations in 1920 and during the Spanish conflict passed a series of neutrality acts making it illegal for Americans to sell or transport war materials to other nations – a position championed by the celebrity aviator Charles Lindbergh, who would soon after become chairman of the isolationist America First Committee. At the same time, Congress looked the other way as American corporations such as Texaco Oil, Ford, Studebaker, General Motors and DuPont supplied 12,000 trucks, fuel and bombs to Franco's forces, along with easy credit to pay for them. This gave Franco's army the mobility necessary to fling his better-armed forces against one Republican offensive after another.

The Republic, meanwhile, was forced to rely on enthusiastic but mostly untrained and ill-armed international volunteers, as well as aid from the Soviet Union. The latter required the Republicans to cede political and military policy to Stalin.

Spanish democracy could exist on idealism and morale and élan for only so long. It needed arms to win the war, but the diffident Western democracies continually refused to supply them.

George Orwell, who would join the fighting at the end of 1936, said: 'The outcome of the Spanish war was settled in London, Paris, Rome, Berlin – at any rate not in Spain . . . The Fascists won because they were the stronger; they had modern arms and the others hadn't.'

What could convince the democracies to change their minds and arm democracy before it was too late?

◊

Nothing, apparently.

On 14th August, just four weeks after the start of the civil war, General Juan Yagüe's Francoist forces, which had been advancing northwards, breached the walls of the Republican-held city of Badajoz. For four days the world knew nothing of what happened there, but on 18th August, reports that seemed hard to believe began appearing in European newspapers. The victorious troops had gone on a medieval rampage through the streets, killing anyone suspected of supporting the Republicans. Militiamen, civilians, children – all fell in huge numbers. Eyewitnesses saw hundreds of dead lining the streets where they had fallen. Some suggest a thousand people were killed this way. Those who survived the massacre were concentrated in the Plaza de Toros, where, that night, firing squads with machine guns began their work, killing off the prisoners in batches before transporting their bodies by truck to the city cemetery, where they were burned.

How many were murdered that day and night: 2,000? 4,000? Nobody can agree. But there are three things of which we can be certain. First, shooting squads, common in the Soviet Union, had arrived in Western Europe. Second, human bodies were now being burned. Third, the price for allowing populism to spread throughout Europe was war – as Keynes had warned. The leaders of the Western democracies didn't care enough to do the only thing that at this point could have halted the slide to a wider war: arm the forces of democracy or intervene directly.

◊

Maybe something else – like the bombing of cities – might make them wake up.

On Monday, 26th April 1937, exhausted Republican troops and refugees fell back on the regional city of Guernica, which stood in the way of General Emilio Mola's advance into the Basque region. The city was packed with vulnerable humanity. At 4.30 p.m. the church bells rang an air raid warning. A single bomber of the German Condor Legion – the air wing Hitler had sent to Spain to test his air warfare tactics – dropped its load on the centre of town, which was then strafed by fighter bombers. Some forty-five minutes later, three more squadrons of bombers carpet-bombed the town in twenty-minute relays that went on for two and a half hours. By the time they had finished their mission, the centre of the defenceless town was in flames and ruins, and many hundreds of its mostly civilian inhabitants were dead.

The world soon found out what had happened. The next morning, the destruction of the revered city of the Basques was reported in the world press. Picasso's famous painting of the war crime would later cause a sensation that ensured the whole world understood populism's endpoint. Another dark portent of the near future had arrived.

Something more than the bombing of cities had also arrived: disinformation. General Franco's propaganda machine spread the lie that the Republicans had burned Guernica down themselves in what we would now call a false flag operation to make their opponents look bad.

Many were taken in. In his August 1942 essay 'Looking Back on the Spanish War', George Orwell said that, in Spain, he had seen 'history being written not in terms of what happened but of what ought to have happened according to various "party lines"'. 'This kind of thing is frightening to me,' Orwell went on, 'because it often gives me the feeling that the very concept of objective truth is fading out of the world.'

The world had started to discover the danger of fake news.

◊

Starved of help by the democracies, the Republic bravely fought on.

On 24th July 1938, the Spanish Republic's 5th and 15th Army Corps crossed the Ebro River and attacked in an attempt to prove to the democracies that the Republic was still alive, still capable of offensive operations, its abandonment a black mark on the democratic world's conscience, a stain which might yet be erased. Around the world, supporters of the Spanish Republic held their breath. Maybe, they thought, Britain, France and America would finally end their policy of non-intervention and arm the Spanish democracy as a bulwark against fascism, allowing it to hang on until the now inevitable-looking European war broke out.

At first the offensive worked, liberating hundreds of square kilometres from fascist rule. But within a week, the operation was revealed as a folly. Lacking sufficient trucks, artillery, tanks and aircraft, the Republican forces were at the mercy of their highly mechanised and well-armed opponents. On the exposed rocky plains and hills of the open battleground, they were pounded by plentiful, modern German artillery and aircraft and confronted by fresh troops rushed to the front by the thousands of trucks American capitalism had supplied. Stubbornly and probably unwisely, the Republican troops hung on until 16th November, when they retreated across the river to their old defensive positions. Their armies were now effectively destroyed. The final Nationalist offensive then commenced, leaving carnage in its wake. On 26th January 1939 Barcelona fell, followed two months later by Madrid and Valencia. On 1st April the war was over. The terms were unconditional surrender. The round-ups and executions accelerated. The concentration camps began to fill up and would remain in operation until Francisco Franco, the last of the 1930s fascist dictators, died in 1975.

The rampant fascist populists had learned a vital lesson: the democracies were weak and would let them get away with anything. It seemed nothing would wake them up to what was coming. The historian Richard J. Evans has concluded that to Hitler the Spanish Civil War was yet another example of British and French spinelessness which convinced him to speed up his plans, quickening the arrival of the Second World War.

CHAPTER 5

CONSEQUENCES

On the morning of 7th November 1938, a Polish Jew named Herschel Grynszpan, incensed because his family had recently been deported from Germany to Poland, walked into the German embassy in Paris and shot its third secretary, Ernst vom Rath, five times. The shooter had chosen an inauspicious moment. Hitler and the Nazi leadership were in Munich preparing for a speech to celebrate the fifteenth anniversary of the Beer Hall Putsch. What better way to mark the occasion than a pogrom – something Reich propaganda minister Joseph Goebbels was keen to see happen. In his eyes, Grynszpan may have only been one Jew, but when a Jew commits a crime, all Jews must be held responsible. Rath hung onto life for nearly two days but died in the late afternoon of 9th November. Upon hearing of his death, Hitler informed Goebbels that the assault should begin. No public orders were to be given, though no obstacles were to be put in the way. With the world watching on, violence must have deniability.

Even at this late point, after five years of Nazi rule, many Jews were surprised when gangs of Stormtroopers started bashing down their doors, smashing anything of worth, hauling the inhabitants out of their beds, beating up the men and sometimes the women, humiliating them in the street, smashing the windows and destroying the stock of their shops and burning down their synagogues. As the synagogues and Jewish shops burned, the local fire brigade aimed their hoses at the houses belonging to the good Germans who lived next door. Officially, ninety-one Jews were murdered, hundreds more arrested, and an estimated 300 committed suicide. Some 520 synagogues were destroyed, along with 7,500 shops. In the week following, 30,000 Jews were rounded up and sent to Dachau and the other concentration camps that had opened since 1933 to handle the overflow: Lichtenburg, Sachsenhausen, Buchenwald and Flossenbürg, where the death rate of the routinely brutalised inmates spiralled.

It is probably hard for us – fortunate possessors of historical hindsight – to comprehend how people could still have been shocked and surprised at such things in November 1938. Hitler had repeatedly made plain his attitude and policies towards the Jews, and the violent, savage political culture of the times was evident to all. But it seems to be part of our nature to think people can't really be serious when they tell us they intend to stray from orthodox, managerial forms of political behaviour. *It's outlandish . . . exaggerated . . . a worst-case scenario dreamed up by the usual doomsayers . . . No, it's never going to happen . . . Please stop scaring everyone.* By late 1938, many of those doubters were absolutely terrified. But it was too late to stop the inevitable.

◊

The failure to wake up to the reality that Hitler was going to do what he said he would do soon had consequences beyond Germany's borders.

As the Spanish Republicans were being beaten back across the Ebro, the emboldened Hitler, having got away with renouncing Germany's Versailles Treaty commitments in 1935, with remilitarising the Rhineland in 1936 and with annexing Austria in March 1938, decided to make a grab for the ethnic German regions of Czechoslovakia.

The irony would not have been lost on Keynes. He had warned the politicians that the anger caused by the Versailles Treaty would unleash dark forces that would undermine the economic basis of European civilisation, weakening the victors as well as the vanquished. Within only twenty years, the populist enemies of civilisation had gained the upper hand. The democracies were short of both weapons and conviction. Their citizens were desperate to avoid another war. And right then, as the reality was sinking in and the weakness of their position was plain to see, Hitler was thumbing his nose at the treaty. Its words were worthless. In fact, they had brought the Nazis to power. And now the treaty would bring another war. In their weakened state, the victors of the First World War fell back on appeasing a man who had already proven himself impossible to appease. A man who looked down upon their open-handed offers of peace in return for restraint with utter contempt, seeing such offers only as confirmation that they would never fight back. At the Munich Conference in September 1938, the British and French had done a deal to give him the Sudetenland of Czechoslovakia in return for promises of no more territorial claims.

Then Hitler took over the rest of Czechoslovakia and turned his eyes on Poland. Just as he said he would.

◊

Everyone at this time was, almost daily, waking up to strange, unsettling surprises. What could have been more surprising than a deal between Nazism and communism? On 23rd August 1939, German foreign minister Joachim von Ribbentrop and Soviet minister of foreign affairs Vyacheslav Molotov had signed the German–Soviet Non-Aggression Pact. If Hitler invaded Poland, Stalin's troops would stay out of it. Secret clauses allocated western Poland to Germany, and eastern Poland, along with Latvia, Lithuania and Estonia, to the Soviet Union. As deals go, this was a killer. And deals, after all, are what authoritarians pride themselves on and brag about endlessly. To the populist politician, 'the deal' is the ultimate expression of their power.

The night before the pact was announced, George

Orwell, staying at a friend's country house, had a dream that the war had started. Hearing the headlines on the BBC over breakfast, he knew instinctively that he would do what he had done in Spain. He would volunteer to fight. Despite the brazenness of the Hitler–Stalin deal, Orwell wasn't surprised by it. Earlier than most writers, he had observed something important. Authoritarians like Hitler and Stalin may have had opposing ideologies, but they were essentially the same beast. They were mutually attracted in the same way that bullies are attracted to each other in a school playground and feel perfectly comfortable doing deals to divide up their turf. *You take the sports oval, and I'll take the basketball court. Deal?* They admire the strong. They are interested in power and celebrate it like a religion. Their true enemies aren't each other, but those who insist on the rule of law. Their methods of obtaining and holding onto power are essentially the same. Above all else, they want to abolish democracy. They respect only one thing: strength. They despise the same thing: weakness. In the absence of strength, they win.

Eventually the price of weakness had to be paid.

◊

On Friday, 1st September 1939, the English poet Wystan Hugh Auden awoke from a bad dream with a headache and a hangover. Two days earlier, he had returned to New York from California on a Greyhound bus whose radio had kept the bored passengers up to date with the final few days of peace in Europe. On 23rd August had come the signing of the Molotov–Ribbentrop Pact. On 25th August, the signing of the Polish–British Common Defence Pact, meaning any German attack on Poland to claim Danzig and the Polish Corridor would trigger war. On 29th August, the Polish mobilisation. And in subsequent days, the various diplomatic dances played themselves out. By the time Auden stared at the front page of the *New York Times* that September morning, the time differences between the American east coast and Europe had allowed the compositors to set, in uppercase type:

GERMAN ARMY ATTACKS POLAND;

CITIES BOMBED, PORT BLOCKADED;

DANZIG IS ACCEPTED INTO THE REICH

BRITISH MOBILIZING

By 4.30 p.m. New York time, the British government had delivered its ultimatum to Germany: withdraw or there will be war. No one was under any illusion as to the outcome. The war had effectively begun. Auden decided to go out drinking.

A cab took him from his 81st Street apartment to the gay pick-up joint where he had got his headache the evening before, the Dizzy Club on 52nd Street, between Fifth and Sixth Avenues. Outside, on the footpath, another radio, this time in a limousine, updated him on the terrible news.

By late evening, the Dizzy Club would be throbbing,

but at this time, late afternoon, it was quiet. And in the hushed surroundings, the shy Auden found himself alone at a corner table. He pulled out his notebook and pen and wrote the first poem of the Second World War, *September 1, 1939,* in which, in memorable opening lines, he describes the thirties as a low, dishonest decade that broke the clever hopes of the world.

Low and dishonest . . . Yes, that sums it up. It had taken less than twenty years and eight months for it all to happen again.

◊

Poland was rapidly overrun and divided up between Nazi Germany and the Soviet Union. The dark, racist and elite-hating heart of populism was now unleashed on the conquered populations. The murder of Poland's Jews and its educated leaders began immediately.

In the opening days of the war, German troops advancing across Poland began systematically massacring villagers to spread terror. Dozens and sometimes hundreds died at a time. Jews were a special target and it took only days for their organised mass murder and forced expulsions into the Soviet-occupied zone to commence. One example provides a foretaste of what was to come. On 4th September, just four days into the war, a detachment of the Einsatzgruppen – the special forces of the SS which had the job of 'pacifying rear areas' – entered the southern Polish city of Będzin, herded its Jews into their synagogue and set it on fire using flamethrowers. Some 500 Będzin Jews died in just two days. The scale and horror were replicated in hundreds of cities, towns and villages across conquered Poland.

Nazi white supremacist ambitions went far beyond the elimination of the Jews. Ethnic Poles – like all ethnic Slavs – were also considered subhuman and potential poisoners of German blood and were expected to serve their new Aryan masters. To render them pliant, their educated leaders were to be eliminated. And to achieve this, the head of Reich security, Reinhard Heydrich, developed 'Operation Tannenberg' – a plan to decapitate the leadership of Poland by murdering 61,000 of its most accomplished citizens.

The closest conquered region, Polish Pomerania, was the first to suffer from this '*Intelligenzaktion*', beginning in the first weeks of the war. Educated Pomeranians of Polish ethnicity were quickly rounded up, tortured and transported to the forests outside the village of Wielka Piaśnica, where they were forced to strip naked and stand in front of wide pits (which they sometimes had first to dig), before they were machine-gunned to death by members of the Einsatzgruppen or local ethnic German volunteers. The still-living were either shot or finished off by a rifle butt to the head. Children were sometimes killed by having their heads smashed against trees. Between 12,000 and 16,000 Polish 'elites' were eliminated in such ways in Pomerania alone in the first months of the war. In 1944, the retreating German army exhumed and burned the bodies in a failed attempt to destroy the evidence.

So it all began.

Like Heydrich, the head of the Soviet NKVD, Lavrentiy Beria, also hated Poles and wanted them dead, especially the Polish officer class. Communists hated elites as much as Nazis did. Beria set out to accomplish it but in a more structured way than his temporary allies had managed, benefiting from lessons learned during Stalin's Terror. By April 1940 he was ready, and the place to start was obvious. Many thousands of Polish officers who had been captured when Poland surrendered in early October 1939 – including some of the nation's most educated professionals – were massed in prisoner-of-war camps at Kozelsk and Ostashkov in Russia and Starobilsk in Ukraine.

The Kozelsk inmates were dealt with first. After being told they were being released, the officer prisoners were transported by bus, thirty at a time, to a resort at the edge of the Katyn forest, where they were surrounded by NKVD guards. After being searched and their valuables stolen, they were taken, one at a time, into the basement of one of the resort buildings, where their hands were tied behind their backs and they were shot in the back of the head. The inmates of the other two camps followed soon after, murdered in the same systematic fashion. Some 15,000 Polish officers were eliminated in this way. When their still decaying bodies were dug up by the Germans in 1943, the Soviets spread the fake news that the Germans had killed them.

In 1945 a surviving Polish officer named Józef Czapski,

who had discovered the fate of his missing comrades, told the story of the massacre to George Orwell, then a war correspondent in Paris, who was again unsurprised. The combination of hatred, mass murder and lies seemed somehow to sum up the spirit of the times.

◊

These mass killings were just the beginning. We now know what followed. Six years of fighting – more if you count the Japanese invasion of Manchuria and China, Mussolini's attack on Abyssinia and the civil war in Spain. The Jewish Holocaust. Countless humans tortured, including children. Mass internment. The greatest displacement of people in human history. Generalised hunger and starvation. Area bombing, with dozens of cities, including their medieval and Renaissance treasures, razed to the ground. The invention of the atomic bomb and its use on Nagasaki and Hiroshima. Some 50 million dead – 22 million soldiers, 12 million concentration camp inmates, 1.5 million bombing victims, 14.5 million other civilians. And grieving millions more left behind, haunted by the memories and ghosts of those they once loved. More concentrated suffering than ever before or since.

The suffering was not evenly shared. Proportionally, the country that suffered the most was Ukraine, with over 7 million of its citizens dead (more than one in six of all Ukrainians), 14.5 million deported or evacuated and 19 million made homeless.

Such were the consequences of letting the populists get the upper hand . . . the first time.

Will we let there be a second?

PART II

FARCE

Our world has changed. We used to be in a postwar world, now we are in a prewar world. That is the change, and it is taking place in people's heads.

– **Ivan Krastev**, *Der Spiegel*, **17 March 2022**

CHAPTER 1

SOWING THE WIND

There's a photograph that, once seen, is hard to get out of your mind. It was taken in the summer of 1945 at one of the popular swimming lakes in Berlin. It is sunny and hot, perfect holiday weather. People are boating. Children are frolicking in the water while their parents watch lazily from the bank. A group of young people, including young women in those pre-bikini swimsuits they wore back then, are lying or standing on their towels, probably just back from a cooling dip. No more than 5 metres from them is the grave of a German soldier, marked by a cross and three army helmets. Even with such evidence so close by, is it possible they may already have started to forget?

◊

Maybe only a little. The second great catastrophe of the century had left even more dead than the first and we seemed to learn its lessons well, and remember them for a long time.

We even changed our world to make its repetition unlikely. Until, of course, we started to forget, and to sow the wind once again.

◊

John Maynard Keynes had not forgotten. In July 1944, as the war he had tried to prevent was ending, he was at another conference of the great powers, engaged in a struggle to ensure that *this time* the groundwork for peace *would* be properly laid. The lessons of the Paris Peace Conference would be learned. History would not repeat. The populists would not return. Another world war would not follow.

His thinking had become more sophisticated in the interwar years. When economic catastrophe had struck in 1929, he had devised a way to repair it – by managing domestic demand to achieve economic stability. The resulting calm, he believed, would inoculate nations against populist demagogues. The civilised values he so cherished would survive. Now he was determined that the stability his policies had brought to individual nations would be brought to the world.

For this second grand conference of his lifetime, Paris was replaced by the New Hampshire suburb of Bretton Woods. Delegates from forty-four countries met to thrash out a system of cooperation to support nations under economic pressure (the sort of pressure that had produced the trade barriers, devaluation, paper money printing, hyperinflation and mass unemployment that had led to 1939). Keynes' own detailed proposal was defeated by that of Harry Dexter White from the US Treasury, but the system adopted was strongly imbued with his belief in a rules-based international financial order to support stable currencies and thus the growth of trade and prosperity. To do this, the system pegged currencies to the US dollar, and created two bodies: the International Monetary Fund to provide international credit and the International Bank for Reconstruction and Development (later part of the World Bank) to provide development loans.

Suffering from bacterial endocarditis (which can today be treated by antibiotics), Keynes died, exhausted, in April 1946. But his work was done.

◊

Keynes' theories helped restore stability to a world destroyed by a second major war. US loans under the Marshall Plan financed the rebuilding of Europe. For the next thirty years, incomes rose steadily – in Europe even more so than in America, where the starting point for standards of living was higher. More importantly, that growth was shared. As Australian politician and economist Andrew Leigh put it:

> Across the advanced world, jobs were plentiful, wages rose faster than profits, and earnings rose faster on the factory floor than in the corner office . . . The French called the three post-war decades *les Trente Glorieuses*. The Italians referred to *il boom economico*. The Spanish dubbed it *el milagro económico español* (the Spanish

economic miracle). Germans called it *das Wunder am Rhein* (the Miracle on the Rhine).

All classes prospered, enjoying a standard of living their parents never knew. The old demons of unemployment, fascism, German militarism, war and revolution disappeared. The ideal of a peaceful, cooperative Europe was born and what we now know as the European Union began to take shape. Politicians, who recalled the political extremism of their youth, gravitated towards the middle ground. Social democracy had its great moment. Social reforms were implemented and new institutions built. In Western Europe, at least, the putsches, riots, massacres, assassinations, pogroms and wars survived only in memory. In Eastern Europe, the hatreds of the war persisted longer but a grey solidity slowly took hold as living standards crept up and political repression moderated. In short, populism was defeated by a stable, shared affluence that managed to last.

◊

Until, that is, history faded into the past and memories began to fail. Especially the memories of the economists.

Because when the economists forgot, it all started to unravel again. Unemployment rose. Inequality widened alarmingly. Civilisation's enemies once again found audiences willing to listen to them. A new age of populism eventually returned. The angry, ranting conspiracists, whose heroes had been killed off at the end of the Second World War, could once again step from the shadows into the light.

◊

We can now see what happened. A new global economic order was coming into being as Asian development took off. Simultaneously, a new ideology that championed lower taxes, smaller government, weaker labour unions and diminished welfare took hold almost everywhere. Too little was done to ameliorate the devastating effect of this economic transformation on the living standards of the working class. Across America and Europe, factories were flattened, unions shrank, communities were abandoned, generations-long ways of working and living were destroyed. To take one prominent example, the US city of Detroit, which had employed hundreds of thousands of auto workers half a lifetime earlier, became a decaying, crime- and drug-ridden museum whose population fell by 25% between 2000 and 2010. The American Midwest's steel and mining towns, like those of the British Midlands and north, endured generation-long recessions, becoming bywords for drug and alcohol abuse and early death for the working class, whose life expectancy fell.

The story was replicated in many industrial areas across Europe. Their political bases destroyed, social-democratic parties saw their vote plummet. Once-proud political movements lost their sense of purpose, and, inevitably, insurgent parties and leaders arose from the fringes to speak for the dispossessed and make them their own. In the United States between 1977 and 2007, the wealthiest 10% of the population grabbed 75 per cent of the growth, with the wealthiest 1 per cent taking 60 per cent. The bottom 90 per cent increased their income by less than 0.5 per cent a year. In Britain, the top 10 per cent of income earners increased their share of income from 27 per cent in 1970 to 43 per cent in 2010. In France and Germany, the trend was in the same direction, though less extreme. By the time people realised the long-term political consequences of this widening inequality it was too late to turn back.

Europe and America were again learning Keynes' point that, outside Asia at least, 'neither capitalism nor liberalism could survive very long without one another'. Soon, people were looking for 'others' to blame. This time maybe not Jews (at least not yet), but Muslims, Africans, Pakistanis, Mexicans, Latin Americans and anyone else easy to accuse of stealing their jobs, imposing their own culture and bringing crime. And in the face of their feeling of dispossession and betrayal by the political class, ordinary people looked elsewhere for leadership and sought revenge. The mouthers of managerial slogans were out. 'Plain speakers' and strongmen who were willing to help even the score were back in demand.

As had happened a century earlier, the populist disaster began in the East.

◊

In Russia, the replay of the past came with a 'Shok'.

Shock therapy was the policy of Yegor Gaidar, minister of finance and later first deputy prime minister of Russia under Boris Yeltsin. John Maynard Keynes would most likely have regarded shock therapy as the absolute last economic policy Russians needed just then.

Just months before this 'therapy' commenced, a failed putsch of communist hardliners led by the alcoholic Gennady Yanayev had ended the more-than-eighty-year history of the Soviet Union. (Failed putsches seem to have a way of inciting far-reaching trouble.) Decades of one-party dominance ended abruptly. The state, along with its regulated economy and society, was suddenly toppled. A highly unsatisfactory but (coercively) ordered and settled way of life gave way to anarchy. The historical lessons of the previous century should have been obvious. But Yegor Gaidar was an economist, not a historian, and knew better. In a short time, price regulation was abolished, industrial subsidies were cut, the budget deficit was reduced and publicly owned enterprises privatised – or, in effect, stolen – by giving people 'vouchers' that were eventually gobbled up by those we now call the oligarchs.

Free-market economists naturally argue that there was no alternative. In the lead-up to the 'Shok', while the Soviet Union was disintegrating, oil prices and production had plummeted, the deficit had ballooned, the gold reserves had been sold off, domestic prices had risen, there was rampant inflation and food supply problems, and street crime had gone up. But the cure was in some ways worse than the disease. For the people, their problems were nothing compared to the miseries they were about to endure.

The misery came in the form of our old friend hyperinflation. Between January and December 2002, inflation in Russia shot up from 200 per cent to nearly 2600 per cent. A kilo of meat cost more than three weeks of a primary school teacher's salary. Intellectuals – former high-status professors – were reduced to living on noodles, with potatoes and bread considered luxuries. Salaries went unpaid, though people stayed in their jobs anyway to be part of a new barter economy and seek safety in a community they knew. The dead (now more numerous) were sometimes buried wrapped in old newspapers and plastic bags because wooden coffins were unaffordable and, without being paid, doctors wouldn't sign the death certificates necessary for burial in a cemetery. Criminal gangs wearing combat fatigues and gold chains roamed the streets with military weapons, having bribed the police and the judges to turn a blind eye or even to help them. Those with country dachas retreated to them to grow food in their gardens. Those who stayed behind installed steel doors to keep themselves safe. Marauding mafia gangs could arrive and steal people's homes, forcing them at gunpoint to hand over the title and live on the street. During the 1990s Russia suffered the highest per-capita suicide rate in the world. Life expectancy fell by eight years for men and two and a half years for women as people starved, died in shootings, drank themselves to death or overdosed on drugs. According to Leigh, since the fall of communism, 99% of Russia's growth has gone to the top 10% of income earners, and Russia today is probably less equal than before the Bolshevik Revolution.

This 'wild capitalism', as Russians called it, bewildered people used to the stasis of the Soviet Union since the early 1960s. Their ideas, their education, their books, their status all became worthless as the world was given over to a new elite of spivs and crooks and prostitutes, ferrying themselves around Moscow in shiny Mercedes limousines, protected by corrupt policemen or mafia toughs.

While this was going on, violence broke out between national minorities within the newly independent states of the former Soviet Union. Armenia and Azerbaijan fought over Nagorno-Karabakh; Abkhazia, South Ossetia and Adjara sought to leave Georgia; and Chechnya tried to secede from Russia. The latter conflict produced two full-scale wars in which the Chechen capital, Grozny, was razed and tens of thousands of people were killed (no one can agree a total figure) – including 186 children and 148 adults in an infamous primary school hostage siege in the North Ossetia town of Beslan in 2004. Those who thought the hatreds and killing of the 1940s could never return to Europe were proved wrong.

But Gaidar and his self-styled 'economic kamikaze team', whose dream was to create capitalism in 500 days, never regretted a thing and never expected to be thanked.

When, afterwards, he fell out with his country's leader, Gaidar came down with a mysterious and unexplained illness while travelling overseas.

◊

Into this chaotic world stepped the strongman everyone now craved. A virtual nobody. Someone capable of providing stability and leadership. Someone with an innate grasp of how to appeal to the masses. His name was Vladimir Putin.

Putin was first appointed prime minister on 31st December 1999 by the ailing President Boris Yeltsin, whose supporters thought the newcomer a nondescript but useful tool of their interests. Soon after, though, Putin was elected in a landslide. Faced with economic turmoil and lacking mature democratic institutions, Russia's citizens willingly surrendered their fleeting post-Soviet political freedoms to a man whose character they didn't really know, but whose dictatorial inclinations they likely suspected from his time as an agent of the KGB (successor organisation to the NKVD) and as director of the Federal Security Service (FSB) (which in turn had succeeded the KGB). Around the world, those who had hailed the birth of Russian democracy and freedom after the end of the Soviet Union were surprised at how quickly this capitulation to authoritarianism had occurred, but they shouldn't have been. History had already demonstrated that economic shocks have a way of bringing democracy undone.

CHAPTER 2

POPULISM

Meanwhile, in the capitalist West, groups of self-styled intellectuals, easily dismissed as harmless cranks, were busy creating the ideology for a new, stridently *völkisch* populist movement that would, in little more than a decade, be poised to challenge and overturn the world order. It became known as the alt-right – an online-based anti-liberal, anti-feminist, nativist and white supremacist successor movement to 1930s fascism, Nazism and Stalinism. Linked by the internet and social media, its various components quickly assembled into a recognisable global alliance.

From France came this new movement's prime animating philosophy. In 2010 the fringe conspiracy theorist Renaud Camus coined a catchy new term – 'the Great Replacement' – for a not-so-new idea: that elite policymakers around the world were conniving to replace established white populations, their cultures and their civilisations with immigrants from the Global South. In an era of popular outrage over cross-border refugee flows, this idea – the movement's lightly disguised racist core – found willing audiences everywhere. In no time, on the streets of America as elsewhere, white supremacists were marching side by side, chanting their angry new slogan: 'You will not replace us. You will not replace us. You will not replace us'. The Nazi idea of Aryan supremacy had been given a new guise.

From Germany came the movement's electoral renaissance. The Alternative for Germany party (AfD), launched in 2013, demonstrated that even in a country where Nazism is expressly prohibited, a support base for carefully reformulated *völkisch* ideas can still be found – one big enough to rival the established mainstream parties. Its major targets today? Syrian refugees and the European Union.

From Hungary came populism's governing strategy. Having regained power in 2010 after an eight-year spell in opposition, Viktor Orbán's Fidesz party developed a successful *modus operandi* for the gradual creation of an illiberal (or anti-liberal) state. Its operating principle? Stealth. Its means? Stacking the judiciary, gerrymandering electoral boundaries, controlling the media and, slowly but surely, legislating away free speech and individual freedoms. Its message? A drumbeat of nativism, Christian traditionalism and barely disguised racism and antisemitism. (The Jewish billionaire financier and philanthropist George Soros is Fidesz's Enemy Number 1.) Its goal? To challenge democracy at every turn, destroy the European Union and the United Nations, win national culture wars for the right and make liberal freedoms a thing of the past. Orbán quickly became the poster boy of the American and European right, including those inside the mainstream centre-right parties. His approach was widely discussed at Conservative Political Action Conferences across the world. Who knows where such a governing strategy might lead? As Orbán himself said: '[T]he essence of the future is that anything can happen. And it is difficult to define "anything".'

From Britain the movement got its first big shot of confidence. In June 2016 a nativist campaign led by a hard-edged campaigner (Nigel Farage) and a charismatic, conservative, privileged populist (Boris Johnson) achieved Brexit against the combined opposition of the official leadership of the mainstream parties, and sent a shiver down the spine of the democratic world. *Such things can happen in Britain?*

And from America, populism got confirmation of its ability to take power by democratic means in the most powerful nation on Earth.

◊

To win in America, the movement needed a media-savvy campaign strategist: a master of the latest campaign techniques, someone totally loyal to the cause, battle-hardened, willing to overturn all existing methods and operate free of all moral constraints. In other words, it needed a committed revolutionary willing to tear down the political system and replace it with something completely new. Such a person existed. His name was Steve Bannon.

Surprisingly (or perhaps not) for a leader of the alt-right, Bannon's role model was the leader of the Bolshevik Revolution, Vladimir Ilyich Lenin. Lenin, he said, 'wanted to destroy the state and that's my goal too. I want to bring everything crashing down and destroy all of today's establishment.' If he *could* destroy the establishment (which he called the 'uniparty'), he believed his alt-right movement might rule for a hundred years.

The makings of Bannon's revolution were already in place. He had shock troops – thousands of bored and alienated young men linked to each other via internet message boards. And he had a propaganda machine – his Breitbart News channel and later his aptly named podcast, *The War Room*. All he needed for success was an appealing front man to act as leader.

◊

On 16th June 2015 real estate tycoon and reality TV star Donald J. Trump, having been introduced by his glamorous daughter Ivanka, descended a golden escalator in Trump Tower in New York, took to a podium in front of a water wall and, before an electric-blue billboard bearing his name and the words MAKE AMERICA GREAT AGAIN!, announced that he would be running for president. Several dozen people looked on. Some were just plain curious.

Others were obviously bewildered. And yet others were there because they'd been paid $50. He made a wild speech, bragging about his wealth and the goodness of his personality, and warning the world about the danger posed by Mexican rapists. It was all somewhat extreme and strange and pathetic. Some of the junior journalists present (the senior ones had been sent to cover more important events) wondered whether he would garner enough support to qualify for the televised Republican primary debates.

◊

One of those watching the golden escalator descent on TV was Steve Bannon, who thought to himself: 'That's Hitler.' Bannon saw immediately that this candidate understood the aesthetics of power and was someone who 'can make himself a vessel for America's grievances and desires'.

◊

Like other populists before him, Trump needed something more to get his revolution over the line: the backing of a willing media tycoon. Fortunately, one was to hand. Over several decades, Australian-American mogul Rupert Murdoch had built a print and television news empire whose method – reinforced through his constant interference in editorial decisions – was to sow discord, create an atmosphere of catastrophe and chaos, and convince the common person that educated, left-wing elites were fools, enemies and traitors. His high-circulation newspapers and Fox News channel polarised opinion, in part by promoting authoritarian conspiracy theories and creating a widespread sense of rudderlessness, to which the only viable answer could be a strong and implacable leader.

At first even Rupert Murdoch refused to take the brash, clownish upstart Donald Trump seriously. But once Trump appeared set to win the Republican presidential nomination, Murdoch's media empire warily swung behind him.

◊

In the lead-up to the November 2016 election, Trump made Bannon his campaign director. Bannon pulled the strands together to give discontented Americans a simple message to believe in ('Make America Great Again'), enemies to focus their dark hatred upon (migrants, the Chinese, liberal elites and the Democratic candidate, 'Crooked Hillary' Clinton), and a fearless leader to vote into power. Trump's campaign was built around huge rallies that generated energy and momentum with powerful, well-honed messages.

This type of political campaign was unusual. But maybe we'd seen it before? It had no conventional political programme but was instead a crusade. It wasn't so much about a change of government, but rather chaos, revenge and national redemption. In an era when many millions of

Americans were not sharing in the nation's wealth and power, it was a potent message – one the timid managerialists and technocrats of the opposing side had trouble countering.

◊

Cleveland, 22nd July 2016. Donald Trump, having won the primary campaign, addresses the Republican National Convention in the city's 20,000-seat basketball arena. Thirty million more watch on TV. The stage is festooned with American flags, and behind the podium his giant digital image looks down on the crowd. He accepts the party's nomination for the presidency and gets down to business. It is hot, he is sweating profusely and he knows what the crowd of forgotten, angry people have come to hear.

There's nothing particularly new about today's speech, which is waiting on his autocue. With the help of market research and the best speechwriters he can buy, he has built it up, line by line, each point guaranteed to get the sort of response he wants – cheering, booing, calls for revenge or worse. The chant builds up: 'U-S-A, U-S-A, U-S-A . . .' It is the very definition of a nationalist chant, literally no more than the name of the country. Delivered with a heavy, guttural emphasis on the 'U', it is jarring, crushing, deafening, like the noise of one of the metal presses in Cleveland's closed-down steel mills.

'These are the facts,' says Trump.

Decades of progress made in bringing down crime are now being reversed by this administration's rollback of criminal enforcement. Homicides last year increased by 17 per cent in America's fifty largest cities. That's the largest increase in twenty-five years. In our nation's capital, killings have risen by 50 per cent. They are up nearly 60 per cent in nearby Baltimore. In the president's hometown of Chicago, more than 2000 have been the victims of shootings this year alone. And more than 3600 have been killed in the Chicago area since he took office.

The facts continue. Are they true? The crowd doesn't care. His carefully chosen statistics express what the audience thinks to be true in a country they believe is being taken away from them. Here is a man who seems to understand what they've lost: dependable manufacturing jobs, economic security, their homes, their pride – for some, their feeling of racial superiority. He may be rich, but he is also unafraid, unrestrained and coarse. It is a winning combination.

Now he gets down to business. Attacking 'the other'.

'The number of police officers killed in the line of duty has risen by almost 50 per cent compared to this point last year. Nearly 180,000 illegal immigrants with criminal records, ordered deported from our country, are tonight roaming free to threaten peaceful citizens.'

The crowd jeers.

'The number of new illegal immigrant families who have crossed the border so far this year already exceeds the entire total from 2015.'

The crowd stands and starts shouting: 'BUILD A WALL! BUILD A WALL! BUILD A WALL!'

He waits for them to settle.

'They are being released by the tens of thousands into our communities with no regard for the impact on public safety or resources.'

'BUILD THAT WALL, BUILD THAT WALL, BUILD THAT WALL . . .'

Now they are ready.

One such border-crosser was released and made his way to Nebraska. There, he ended the life of an innocent young girl named Sarah Root. She was twenty-one years old and was killed the day after graduating from college with a 4.0 grade point average. Top of her class. Her killer was then released a second time, and he is now a fugitive from the law. I've met Sarah's beautiful family. But to this administration, their amazing daughter was just one more American life that wasn't worth protecting.

The boos begin.

'One more child to sacrifice on the altar of open borders . . . We are going to build a great border wall to stop illegal immigration, to stop the gangs and the violence, and to stop the drugs from pouring into our communities.'

The crowd erupts. 'BUILD THE WALL, BUILD THE WALL, BUILD THE WALL . . .' Their response is primordial, like sheep bleating in the presence of a wolf claiming to protect them.

He moves on to his opponent, his words at times drowned out by the eager chants of the crowd: 'LOCK HER UP, LOCK HER UP, LOCK HER UP . . .' Time moves slowly, his speech is long, he digresses from the scrolling lines, and sweats even more.

> Big business, elite media and major donors are lining up behind the campaign of my opponent because they know she will keep our rigged system in place. They are throwing money at her because they have total control over everything she does. She is their puppet, and they pull the strings.
>
> That is why Hillary Clinton's message is that things will never change. My message is that things have to change – and they have to change right now. Every day I wake up determined to deliver for the people I have met all across this nation that have been neglected, ignored and abandoned.
>
> I have visited the laid-off factory workers, and the communities crushed by our horrible and unfair trade deals. These are the forgotten men and women of our country. People who work hard but no longer have a voice.

His press secretary has typed the next line in caps in the transcript: 'I AM YOUR VOICE.'

He reaches the end, juts out his jaw and stands before his people. Like the other populists before him, his mission is to fulfil the people's heartfelt desires.

They repay him with their love and fealty: 'U-S-A, U-S-A, U-S-A . . .'

◊

Trump fails to win a majority of votes, but makes sure he has a majority where it counts – the Electoral College, the media, the streets and, later, the Supreme Court. He gains power.

◊

Washington, DC, Wednesday, 6th January 2021. Donald Trump's chaotic presidency, strewn with the unnecessary deaths of hundreds of thousands of Covid-19 victims, was coming to an end. Outside the Capitol building someone had erected a wooden gallows with a neon orange rope. It was meant for Speaker of the House Nancy Pelosi and Vice President Mike Pence, and maybe others.

Meanwhile, 3 kilometres away, outside the White House, President Donald Trump, in black woollen coat and gloves against the cold winter temperatures, stood at a podium before a large bulletproof screen. He was angry. Security had cordoned off the area in front of him, which people could only enter by passing through metal detectors.

Guns, knives and other weapons had been discovered in the crowd throughout the city that day. The FBI and the local police had heard there might be violence. Intelligence had told them that militia organisations were aiming to make a show of it. QAnon, the Proud Boys, the Oath Keepers, the Three Percenters and, having travelled far, the Florida-based Guardians of Freedom had come to town. Probably others too. But despite Trump's increasingly annoyed requests that the metal detectors be switched off and the militia members be allowed within the cordon to hear him, the police wouldn't relent. 'I don't fucking care that they have weapons,' someone overheard him say. 'Let my people in.' After all, they weren't there to shoot *him*.

They were all in Washington because he asked them to come. Three weeks earlier he had tweeted: 'Big protest in D.C. on January 6th. Be there, will be wild!' His goal? To stop the joint sitting of Congress certifying the result of the election he had lost to Joe Biden, to buy time for state legislatures to declare their states' votes tainted and replace their slates of electors to the Electoral College with people who would install him instead.

It was another long and mostly unscripted speech, but the crowd was excited. They'd been aroused by the warm-up acts – including Trump's lawyer, Rudolph Giuliani, who had just told them to seek 'trial by combat'. Trump reminded them, again, that the election had been stolen – a fiction concocted in the weeks leading up to election day by his co-conspirators, including Steve Bannon. Then he got to the point. He told them to walk down to the Capitol, 'Because you'll never take back our country with weakness. You have to show strength and you have to be strong. We have come to demand that Congress do the right thing and only count the electors who have been lawfully slated . . .' Their aim was to intimidate Congress into overturning the result of the presidential election. Insurrection, treason, putsch . . . call it what you will.

The crowd then headed to the Capitol. Trump wanted to join them but his security detail wouldn't allow it. So he sat in his dining room and watched it unfold live on TV. The mob pushed through the flimsy first lines of police barriers, then smashed its way into the building, severely beating guards, before making its way to the chambers, looking for Pelosi and Pence. History was repeating: violent militias were *inside* the legislature, making the people's will clear, threatening murder. At this point, Trump tweeted that 'Mike Pence didn't have the courage to do what should have been done to protect our country and our constitution . . .' Word spread and a chant began: 'HANG MIKE PENCE!' Guns were drawn at the door of the House. A protester was shot dead in the inner corridors. Three more died as a result of the insurrection, one of them a police officer.

But the ragtag putsch soon petered out. Trump, under pressure from his supporters and family, including media backers who had foolishly encouraged his claim that the election was stolen, was forced to thank the mob and send it home. Soon the armed force of the state would descend. The shambles collapsed. As the mob melted away from the Capitol, angry orators sought small audiences among the stragglers. One told them to go back to their homes, make lists of the corrupt traitors and hunt them down. 'Invade your own state capital buildings,' another said. A third yelled out that what they had needed was 30,000 guns. To which someone replied: 'Next time.'

A curfew was activated and the National Guard was called out. Trump continued into the evening, trying to get his supporters in Congress to stop the certification, but it was over. For now.

◊

Rupert Murdoch had a big problem. On election night, his Fox News channel had correctly called the swing state of Arizona for Joe Biden, rendering unviable Trump's intended strategy of declaring victory before the pre-poll votes were counted. Trump was livid and declared war on Fox News. In the weeks that followed, Murdoch discovered something he hadn't foreseen: Fox News' audience no longer belonged to him. It was now loyal first and foremost to Trump. Murdoch's front-page headlines and editorials ridiculing Trump's 'stolen election' claim had no effect. Without Trump's support, Fox's ratings and revenues started to dive. Some of Fox's most popular news presenters jumped ship or were forced out. Murdoch now needed Trump more than Trump needed Murdoch – as always seems to be the way when you let a scorpion ride to power on your back. Insiders reported that the nonagenarian Murdoch wished Trump was dead.

◊

The mob may have just come for them with its clubs and guns and gallows and calls for retribution, but inside Congress, 147 Republicans, including future presidential aspirants, still voted to overturn the presidential election. They were scared. They knew their party was not the Grand Old Party any longer. Not the party of Nixon and Reagan and Bush. Not the party of the establishment. It was Trump's party. He now directed its mob like a Stormtrooper directing a flamethrower. Just like Murdoch's news empire, the Republican leaders failed to stand up to Trump when they had the chance and now they were paying the price. They thought they had hired him; that he was their man; that they could push him into a corner, keep him in check, maybe even make him squeak; and now they realised, finally, just how short-sighted they had been. Complicit in their own destruction, they found themselves rendered irrelevant, terrified, the butt of ridicule.

After the putsch failed, just two Republicans served on the House select committee investigating the January 6 attack: Adam Kinzinger and Liz Cheney. This despite the fact that Trump's armed mob had just been inside the building looking to kill several elected representatives.

The cowardice was disturbing and an ill-omen for the future. In 1933, SPD Reichstag deputies had shown far greater courage. Kinzinger soon realised that his days in Congress were numbered and retired. Despite being the daughter of former vice president Dick Cheney, and therefore Republican aristocracy, Liz Cheney was removed from her House Republican leadership position and challenged in the primaries by Trump loyalists. She was smashed by forty points in a vicious and ugly campaign. Those, like House minority leader Kevin McCarthy, who briefly stuck their heads above the trench to criticise Trump's attempted insurrection were quickly forced to recant. The episode made it clear that the only people who could hold office in the GOP anymore were those loyal to Donald Trump, who would uphold the bald lie that the election had been stolen. Establishment conservatism had been almost completely replaced by populist radicalism. The party of constitutionalism and the rule of law had given way to a party of revenge, street mobs and the rule of one man.

◊

Modern Hollywood loves to remake classic movies. And why not, when people seem to forget the old ones so easily? Maybe one day a great Hollywood producer might remake *Cabaret*. If so, there will be no way they can cut out Brian's final question to Max about whether he still thinks he can control the Nazis.

◊

The January 6 insurrection had exposed Trump's dangerous intentions but also his lack of thorough preparation. But that was then. What about next time? And what about future presidential candidates? Will a more merciless and thorough reactionary populist leader arise? Someone with the ruthlessness and strategic sense of Viktor Orbán? Will Trump's example inspire a new alt-right American putschist with a greater capacity to follow through?

Initially, at least, there was hope Trump could be defeated as a political force. In the wake of the failed putsch, the state rallied. He was impeached by the Democratic-controlled House of Representatives, and an impeachment trial for incitement of insurrection followed in the Senate. Success would have prevented Trump from ever again contesting the presidency. But the Senate trial failed to gain the necessary two-thirds majority, despite seven Republican senators voting to convict. Steve Bannon, however, was indicted for contempt of Congress, and the highest-profile and most dangerous militia leaders and members were found guilty of crimes and imprisoned. Over 1,350 other insurrection participants were charged with federal crimes stemming from the attack; nearly 900 were found guilty and around 500 were jailed.

The House select committee published a devastating report that accused Trump of attempted insurrection and recommended his prosecution. As Representative Cheney put it: 'President Trump summoned the mob, assembled the mob and lit the flame of this attack.' On 6th August 2023 the House issued an indictment. Trump was also charged with election interference by the state of Georgia and for mishandling sensitive documents after leaving office. And on 30th May 2024 he was found guilty of falsifying business records to cover up a sexual encounter with an adult film star, Stormy Daniels, in the lead-up to the 2016 election, thus subverting campaign finance laws. Maybe, just maybe, some began to think, the law might catch up with him before he returned to power.

And yet we wonder: is it all moving too slowly? By effectively delaying trials until after the election, are the Supreme Court and other courts making a mistake they might one day regret? Would Trump have given his liberal opponents the same leeway they had given him?

Donald Trump, meanwhile, plays a tried and tested hand. He rounds on those in the media and politics who refuse to support him. He exploits his criminal and civil trials to gain publicity and claim that he is being persecuted for trying to make America great again, hoping that if and when it all comes to a head in the courts, friendly right-wing judges (including some he appointed himself) will delay and delay and maybe let him off. Does he calculate it will make his backstory, his myth – the man who rose above persecution for the good of America – even more impressive? After all, such things have happened before.

As the 2024 election approaches, he doubles down on

his messages. He says he will 'root out the communists, Marxists, fascists and the radical-left thugs that live like vermin within the confines of our country'. He accuses immigrants of 'poisoning the blood' of the nation. He plans a mass deportation of millions of undocumented people and wouldn't rule out the creation of new migrant detention camps – in effect, concentration camps – for those swept up for expulsion. He calls his enemies 'traitors' and threatens to prosecute his presidential opponent and his family. He proposes to clean out federal agencies, including the national security services, removing his opponents and replacing them with 'patriots' to 'shatter the deep state'. He aims to put the presidency above the law by claiming blanket immunity for everything a president does. He has worked with right-wing think tanks to prepare an 887-page post-election playbook titled Project 2025 to ensure that, next time, nothing will be left to chance, and the democratic state will be prevented from foiling his extreme plans. Should he win, he has said, he will be a dictator for a day, and that it will possibly be the last election America ever has. His intention? To leave the defenders of democracy shocked, overwhelmed, completely bowled over, making any form of resistance impossible. No one hearing his tirades could possibly be in any doubt about his intentions. And yet . . . it's all said so flippantly . . . and offhandedly . . . that many think he can't possibly mean it. *He's a fool, it won't be so bad in reality, the laws will constrain him. He'll retract it tomorrow and accuse us of spreading fake news.* If so, it won't be the first time in history such a mistake is made.

Can you see the parallels now?

CHAPTER 3

SAVAGERY

Back in the 1930s Stalin had his show trials. But what need does Vladimir Putin – sometime president, sometime prime minister of the Russian Federation – have of show trials, with their cowed judges whose faux independence fools no one? Where trials are needed to neaten the paperwork, they sometimes happen, but with decisions made away from the cameras. Putin has replaced the show trial with something equally sinister: the show assassination. And these shows are truly spectacular. Because the more spectacular the assassination, the more unmissable the message: *Oppose Putin and you will die.* There are no happy endings for anyone who crosses the Russian leader.

Show Assassination Number 1: Anna Politkovskaya, journalist, October 2006. Her crime? Award-winning reportage on the war in Chechnya and the destruction of Russian democracy. The method? A contract killing in the elevator of her apartment block. Shot in the chest, shoulder and head at close range – after poisoning on an aeroplane flight failed to kill her two years prior. The message? *Don't report the truth.*

Show Assassination Number 2: Alexander Litvinenko, dissident security agent, November 2006. His crime? Spilling the beans on the work of the FSB. He accuses it of planning to murder the television oligarch Boris Berezovsky and outs the regime for staging the Russian apartment bombings of 1999, which Putin used, like the Reichstag fire and Kirov's murder, to play the strongman, win a landslide election and remove individual liberties. The method? Poisoning by the radiotoxic agent polonium-210. Litvinenko's death, including the images of his last days as a bald, doomed hospital patient, caused a sensation, and kept doing so for the next decade. The message? *Don't change sides.*

Show Assassination Number 3: Boris Nemtsov, former deputy prime minister of Russia, February 2015. His crime? Outspoken criticism of Vladimir Putin. Killed while planning a rally against the 2014 Russian war in Ukraine. The method? Shot in the back four times while crossing the Bolshoy Moskvoretsky Bridge, near the Kremlin. The message? *Opposition will not be tolerated.*

Show Assassination Number 4: Yevgeny Prigozhin, businessman and controller of the Wagner militia group, August 2023. His crime? An attempted putsch against the Russian army leadership and Putin himself. The method? A bomb planted on his business jet. The falling aircraft was captured on camera and posted on social media, the better for the world to see. The message? *Revenge will come, sooner or later. Probably sooner.*

Show Assassination Number 5: Alexei Navalny, accepted leader of the Russian democratic opposition through his People's Alliance party and his Anti-Corruption Foundation, February 2024. His crime? Repeatedly uncovering the corruption of the Putin administration, humiliating the regime in the global media and building a popular movement opposing the dictatorship. The method? Probable poisoning or beating while in solitary confinement at the IK-3 'Polar Wolf' penal colony within the Arctic Circle, in the weeks leading up to the March 2024 'election'. The FSB had tried to poison him in a dramatic and widely publicised assassination attempt in 2020. The authorities claim he died from 'sudden death syndrome', which cynics call 'sudden Russian death syndrome'. Like with Trotsky, they needed multiple attempts to terminate him. Navalny was no ordinary dissident, but a global political celebrity and leader. The audacity of his assassination, like that of Prigozhin, was breathtaking – such publicity cannot be bought. The message? *Push democracy and you are dead.*

Here's a thought exercise. Change 'Alexei Navalny' to 'Leon Trotsky', 'People's Alliance' to 'Left Opposition', and 'FSB' to 'NKVD' and the true meaning of Navalny's assassination becomes clear. Change 'Anna Politkovskaya' to 'Nikolai Bukharin', 'Alexander Litvinenko' to 'Genrikh Yagoda', 'Boris Nemtsov' to 'Grigory Zinoviev', 'Yevgeny

Prigozhin' to 'Mikhail Tukhachevsky' and we are back in the Terror of 1937. Reader, we are now getting closer to understanding our times.

◊

On 21st February 2012, members of the punk band Pussy Riot entered the Moscow Cathedral of Christ the Saviour, donned colourful outfits including balaclavas, stood in front of the altar and mock-performed a piece of 'absurdist shock art' called 'Punk Prayer: Mother of God Drive Putin Away'. Like the poems of the Symbolists, Futurists and Acmeists of the revolutionary period, the song is edgy, raw and avant-garde, mocking Russia's leader, this time accusing him of enlisting the church to strengthen his power.

They were quickly stopped and driven out of the cathedral, but posted footage of the performance on the internet soon after. Three members of the band, Maria Alyokhina, Yekaterina Samutsevich and Nadezhda Tolokonnikova, were publicly identified and eventually convicted of 'hooliganism motivated by religious hatred' and sentenced to two years in jail. While Samutsevich was soon released following a successful appeal, the other two stayed in a Russian penal colony for more than a year and a half before being amnestied by Vladimir Putin to soothe Western opinion in the lead-up to the 2014 Sochi Winter Olympics. Two decades after the Communist Party's fall, Russian artists were once again becoming political prisoners. And not just any old prison: Tolokonnikova was incarcerated at IK-14, located in a former part of the Gulag system.

◊

Gradually, controls over culture in Russia began to tighten and writers and artists increasingly felt compelled to leave.

Russian-born American journalist Masha Gessen, who wrote the story of Pussy Riot's persecution, went into exile in the United States after anti-LGBTQ+ legislation made them and their partner fearful for the safety of their young children. Still, though, a degree of artistic freedom remained.

But the crackdown eventually arrived. As the end of 2021 approached, Vladimir Putin, worried about a wave of protests during the recent presidential election, decided dissent had gone too far. Government control was tightened much further – a process that accelerated after the invasion of Ukraine in 2022. Journalists and politicians had already been targeted for imprisonment and execution; now artists could no longer expect to be spared. Provocative plays were banned and their writers detained and threatened with jail sentences of up to seven years. Independent television stations found it impossible to continue broadcasting. Social media couldn't be used freely. Journalists and writers were placed on registers of extremists and terrorists and charged with crimes including 'high treason', 'espionage', 'discrediting the armed forces' or 'spreading false information about the special military operation', some of which attract up to twenty-five years in a penal colony.

In modern Russia, as in the Soviet Union and Nazi Germany, political persecution had morphed, as it always does, into a culture war.

◊

History is speeding up and coming back to us at a frightening pace.

On Friday, 22nd March 2024, several terrorists from Tajikistan connected to the Islamic State terrorist organisation burst into Moscow's Crocus City concert hall and murdered 137 music lovers and injured well over 150 more. Told to kill everyone and show no mercy, they hunted down the terrified victims and shot them at close range with military weapons. Then they threw Molotov cocktails, setting fire to the building and fleeing – but not before trying to lock the main doors in order to burn all those remaining to death.

On the following Monday, after interrogation, four suspects, with swollen, battered faces, were led into prison and charged, the proceedings captured in their full horror by correspondents from the Russian state-owned news agency TASS, Reuters and others.

Dalerdzhon Barotovich Mirzoyev arrived covered in bruises, with a plastic bag around his neck likely used to asphyxiate him. Muhammadsobir Fayzov entered in a wheelchair and seemed to drift out of consciousness as the hearing progressed. One of his eyes was missing. A third suspect, Saidakrami Murodali Rachabalizoda, had his ear covered in gauze. Later, a video circulated showing one of his captors from the Russian military slicing off one of his ears, ramming it into his mouth and instructing him to eat it while others beat him with their rifle butts. The fourth, Shamsidin Fariduni, had earlier appeared in photographs on the internet lying on the floor of a school gym with his pants pulled down around his knees and wires connected to his genitals; the caption read that 80 volts of electricity and water had been applied. These images were proudly shared with the world as if to demonstrate that show trials and show assassinations had now morphed into show interrogations. It was later reported that the interrogator-torturers were connected variously to the FSB, the GRU (the Russian foreign military intelligence agency) and the Wagner paramilitary group, whose members wear the death's head badges of the SS.

Almost laughably, the death penalty is illegal in Russia, banned in a brief moment of liberalism in 1996. It just so happens, though, that the death penalty is still in force in neighbouring Belarus, two of whose citizens died in the Crocus City massacre, and it has been reported that Putin may ensure the men are tried there. The Belarusian method of execution is one we know well: the blindfolded victim is led to a specially created room, where two employees lower him to his knees while a third provides a single pistol shot to the back of the head, NKVD-style. But this Belarusian expedient will only be necessary if Putin fails to reintroduce the death penalty, or the men fail to die unexpectedly in an Arctic prison.

As expected, President Putin tied the terrorists not to Islamic State but to Ukraine, with whom Russia was still at war. A convenient lie. An alternative fact.

The shocking mass murder of innocent people, confessions proudly gained by beatings and torture and widely publicised, bullets to the back of the head . . . The age of savagery our grandparents and great-grandparents endured is back.

CHAPTER 4

PRELIMINARY WAR

Like other populists, Vladimir Putin is surrounded by fringe thinkers of dubious intellectual merit who cherish grand, racialised myths of national regeneration. Putin's only problem is having so many 'make Russia great again' myths to choose from. They're worth listing:

1. Russia was founded as part of the *Kievan Rus* – a great Russian empire that once stretched across modern-day Ukraine, Belarus and European Russia and must be restored.

2. Russia is destined to lead a new Eurasian empire, based on tsarist and Soviet imperial boundaries.

3. Russia is the standard-bearer of a Slavic Orthodox civilisation philosophically compelled to assert itself against the decadent West.

4. Vladimir Lenin, leader of the Bolshevik Revolution, invented fictitious nations like Ukraine and Belarus by legally constituting the Soviet Union as a grouping of independent Soviet republics instead of a unified 'Russian' nation.

5. Joseph Stalin, by contrast with Lenin, was a great man.

The man sometimes referred to as 'Putin's brain', Russian fascist Aleksandr Dugin, potentially holds to all five of these myths – which is perfectly possible using just a smidgen of doublethink. Another useful mythmaker, the novelist Aleksandr Solzhenitsyn, provides an interesting case. After an active life as a dissident anti-communist writer, during which he was arrested, sent to the Lubyanka, imprisoned in the Gulag system for nearly a decade and survived an assassination attempt by the KGB, he converted to the Orthodox religion and ardent pan-Russian nationalism. Solzhenitsyn therefore probably believed 1-4 only. But, in the time-honoured way for artists in Russia, Putin rehabilitated him prior to his death in 2008, cleansed him of his backstory as a human rights advocate and made him into a useful propagandist for his dictatorship.

Were they to be placed in a Venn diagram, theories 1-5 would overlap in one common area with the label: 'Russia must invade Ukraine'.

Just as Hitler, wanting to overturn the Versailles Treaty, found the idea of the Third Reich brilliantly useful, so

Vladimir Putin, wanting to overturn Boris Yeltsin's 1991 relinquishment of Ukraine, couldn't resist the idea of himself as the founder of a New Russia.

◊

In November 2014 Putin began the creation of this New Russia by taking control of two chunks of Ukrainian territory – the Donbas in Ukraine's east and the Crimean Peninsula on the Black Sea. The response of many sounded rather familiar: *Well, you have to admit, he has a point – those regions* do *have majority Russian populations. Let's just hope he doesn't go further. He's said he won't, hasn't he?* Others drew the parallel with what had been said and done when Hitler annexed Austria in 1938.

In July 2021, Putin, confined to the Kremlin by the Covid-19 pandemic, did what dictators always do in such situations: he wrote a long essay justifying his aggressive intentions towards his neighbouring countries – in this case, Ukraine. Russians and Ukrainians, he wrote, were once one people but had been split apart by the deliberate efforts of those who always sought to undermine their unity. Such a tragedy had to be set right. The world therefore shouldn't have been so surprised when, on 24th February 2022, citing threats towards Russian-speaking minorities in Ukraine, he ordered his forces to invade. Large-scale attacks were launched towards Kyiv in the north, Kharkiv in the northeast, the Donbas in the east and Kherson in the south.

◊

But within days it was obvious that the invasion was in trouble. As with the military revolt of the Spanish generals in 1936, the defenders unexpectedly resisted strongly and prevented the Russians from taking the major cities. Like Madrid, Barcelona and Valencia once did, Kyiv, Kharkiv and Odessa stood firm.

◊

A Ukrainian counter-offensive to liberate the outskirts of Kyiv began on 22nd March 2022. On 1st April, Ukrainian troops entered the affluent commuter belt suburb of Bucha, northwest of the city. They found the streets littered with dead bodies, many with their hands tied behind their backs and single gunshot wounds to the head. By 4th April, some 340 corpses had been located – a figure since revised upwards to 458. Five men were found executed in the basement of a children's sanitorium. Some of the dead were under eighteen years of age. Some victims had been raped, their bodies dumped by the roadside, others mutilated in a basement torture centre, yet others beheaded or burned alive. Most had been buried in a hastily dug grave next to the town's St Andrew's Church. Survivors told reporters how they had begged the Russian occupiers to let them bury their loved ones' remains because the dogs were starting to eat them.

It was a similar story in the liberated towns of Irpin and Hostomel. By May, the estimated death count from these three towns was 1,000, of whom 650 appeared to have been shot at point-blank range, NKVD-style. Later, when Izium was liberated, another 440 graves were found, along with credible stories of rape, torture and execution.

Russian foreign minister Sergey Lavrov dismissed the scenes as a stage-managed anti-Russian provocation. Kremlin spokesman Dmitry Peskov said the photographs and videos of the dead bodies were fake. The Russian foreign ministry claimed the evidence had been ordered by the US to sully Moscow's reputation. Once again, the truth no longer seemed to exist. George Orwell's political insights have retained their relevance.

Europe now had new sites of mass murder. A new Badajoz. A new Katyn.

◊

The port city of Mariupol was attacked from land and sea on the opening day of the invasion and, within a week, was encircled and cut off from Ukrainian forces. The defenders – from the tough Azov Regiment, often falsely misrepresented as a neo-Nazi militia – could not be dislodged from their defensive positions. The city was pounded into rubble by aircraft, missiles and artillery as the civilian population hid in basements, suffering from hunger and cold. On 9th March a maternity hospital was bombed, killing dozens of people, including pregnant women. On 16th March the Mariupol Drama Theatre, used as a civilian shelter, was hit, killing many more. Evacuation agreements allowed some of the city's trapped civilians and defenders to escape. Attempts to break the siege failed and the remaining fighters eventually fell back on the Azov iron and steel works, to make a last stand in the complex's underground chambers. The hell of Mariupol's savage Stalingrad-like street fighting continued until 20th May, when the last fighters surrendered, by which time some 90% of the city had been turned to rubble. Human Rights Watch estimated that more than 10,000 people died in the siege. Kharkiv, too, suffered major destruction and deaths.

To its new Badajoz and Katyn, Europe could now add a new Guernica.

◊

The viciousness of the Spanish Civil War eighty-five years ago has returned to Europe. By mid-May 2022, more than 8 million Ukrainians had been internally displaced from their homes, and by late August more than 7 million were living abroad, though many returned home at the earliest opportunity once their cities and towns were liberated. Only in Yugoslavia had this happened to a European nation since the Second World War.

As we saw, the Spanish Civil War of the 1930s was lost not in Spain but elsewhere, when the Western democracies failed to give it arms to defend itself and provide a rebuff to fascist aggression. Would the world learn from this mistake and heed this crucial lesson of history? Would it arm Ukraine and defend international law?

◊

Sometimes, just sometimes, democracies do learn.

Back in February 2022, Russia had expected the war to be over in a matter of days, thinking it would easily take the capital, Kyiv, decapitate the country's leadership and force capitulation. The failure of Putin's *blitzkrieg* allowed the Ukrainians, inspired by their charismatic leader, Volodymyr Zelensky, to regroup, dig in and inflict punishing casualties on the invading forces while pushing them back from the outskirts of Kyiv. Just as in Spain in 1936, a failed seizure of power had started a drawn-out war, and by August, Ukraine had become strong enough to go on the offensive. Its forces recorded stunning victories to the north and east of Kharkiv, liberating more than 74,000 square kilometres of territory. Putin, it seemed, had made a fatal mistake.

In October 2022, after a summer of anticipation, the Ukrainian army broke out of its temporary defensive positions and began a drive to recapture the city of Kherson, on the banks of the Dnipro River near the Black Sea coast. This was a critical moment in the conflict. Situated close to Crimea, Kherson had immense strategic importance, providing a possible staging post for the recapture of that peninsula, illegally annexed by Russia in 2014. But its symbolic importance was even greater. Kherson had been the largest city to fall to the Russians after their invasion of Ukraine on 24th February, and a symbol of Russian victory. Its loss would signal to the world that the war had turned in Ukraine's favour and arming Ukraine was a sensible and potentially winning policy. By 11th November, the Russian forces had abandoned the city and fallen back on a new defensive line on the eastern bank of the Dnipro. Kherson had been liberated. Russia's invasion had turned into an embarrassing disaster.

How had the outnumbered Ukrainian forces pulled off such a stunning reversal against an army considered one of the strongest in the world? Military experts are in general agreement on the two principal causes: the Ukrainians were united and better motivated; and the liberal democracies had armed them with superior weapons. Billions of dollars in aid from Western countries, mostly members of NATO, had given the Ukrainians the battlefield edge, with the most up-to-date anti-tank and anti-aircraft missiles, precision artillery, tanks, armoured personnel carriers, helicopters, drones, infantry weapons and training. Further arms shipments enabled the Ukrainians to prepare a summer offensive in 2023, but while the democratic world looked on, hoping for another set of stunning victories, Russian defences held, resulting in a strategic deadlock similar to that in First World War.

The contrast with the situation that faced the Spanish Republican forces in the Ebro campaign could not have been starker. In 2022 the democracies armed Ukraine with the weapons it needed to fight a fascist-like opponent on equal terms. With the war having entered a stalemate, the question then became: how long would the democracies, with their combined economic and technological superiority to Russia, keep supplying their ally? In the United States especially, could the supporters of Ukraine overcome the isolationism being championed by Putin's populist admirers? Maybe. In April 2024, against strong opposition from pro-Trump Republicans, the US Congress passed a further $61 billion in military and humanitarian aid. Europe also increased its flow of arms. Only time will tell, though, whether the lessons of the 1930s will continue to be adhered to. Will the democracies defeat populism before it becomes too strong, or will they retreat into timidity and fail to call Putin's bluff? The war in Ukraine has become a battle of wills and a measure of our historical understanding.

What will happen? History is watching.

◊

War – the catalyst for revolution. Under its sway, Vladimir Putin's ideological transformation of his empire accelerates.

Every populist dictatorship has its symbol: the swastika, the fasces, the hammer and sickle, huge portraits of Marx, Engels and Lenin. Now, around Russia, a new one appears on the streets: the letter Z. First painted on Russian tanks in Ukraine, giant 'Z' flags appear on apartment blocks,

'Z' posters are pasted on government buildings and schools, and banners bearing the savage symbol of Putin's nationalist aggression and crushing domestic power are carried in parades. Statues of Stalin are a familiar sight once again. Schoolchildren are taught about the former leader's greatness and how to handle AK-47 assault rifles.

In the shadow of the 'Z', the crackdown begins. The last independent television stations are closed. Internet media rebels are hunted down. Books are banned and arrest warrants for their exiled authors are made *in absentia*. Dissidents and anti-war activists are rounded up and start filling the jails. Gay bars are raided and people proposing LGBTQ+ equality are arrested on charges of subverting traditional family values and weakening the nation by promoting moral decay. Members of Pussy Riot have 'Z' painted on their front doors – as a warning. The populist ideology of Putin's dream – a new, aggressively illiberal tsarist-Stalinist Russian empire with links to the Orthodox Church – steadily becomes law. And to make the tsarist-Stalinist analogy complete, constitutional amendments are enacted that will allow Putin, if he so chooses, to rule for life.

CHAPTER 5

CONSEQUENCES

Waco, Texas, Saturday 25th March 2023. Two years and three months have passed since the failed Washington putsch on 6th January. Still the putsch leader walks free. The establishment thinks it has seen him off after his failed presidency, but now Donald Trump is standing again. He takes the stage to announce his second bid for the presidency. Behind him his supporters wave signs – 'Trump 2024' and 'Witch Hunt' – as he rants for what seems an eternity in the warm sunshine.

He wastes no time in outlining who the enemies of the people are: 'the Marxists and communists'; 'the stupid warmongers and the neocons and the RINOs [Republicans in Name Only], the big-money special interests, the open-border fanatics, crazy people'; 'the fake news media'. And he warns them: '2024 is the final battle. That's going to be the big one. If you put me back in the White House, their reign will be over, and America will be a free nation again.' The reckoning is coming.

In 2016 I declared I am your voice. And now I say to you again tonight, I am your warrior. I am your justice . . . And for those who have been wronged and betrayed . . . I am your retribution . . . Either the deep state destroys America, or we destroy the deep state. That's the way it's got to be. You're at a very pivotal point in our country. Either we descend into a lawless abyss of open borders, rampant killings, super hyperinflation . . . and festering corruption. Or we evict Joe Biden from the White House, and we make America great again.

◊

It was as if his speechwriters had been reading histories of the 1920s and '30s.

This is what the future looks like: the past.

◊

25th April 2024, Hungary. Some 3,000 attendees at the Conservative Political Action Committee's global conference in Budapest watch on admiringly as their unofficial leader, Viktor Orbán, takes the stage and addresses the packed, cheering crowd. In the audience are many major figures of the global right-wing populist movement – former and serving presidents and prime ministers, journalists, TV talking heads and opinion columnists. The bulk of Orbán's address is in his native

Hungarian, but at one point he breaks into English: 'Make America great again, make Europe great again! . . . Go Donald Trump! Go European sovereigntists! Let us saddle up, don our armour, take to the battlefield and let the electoral battle begin.'

◊

Twelve days later, 7th May 2024. Vladimir Putin stands defiantly at the Kremlin podium at the inauguration ceremony after his latest presidential victory, which was tainted by electoral manipulation and the murder of Alexi Navalny. Just twenty-four hours before, he had announced that Russia would be holding a tactical nuclear weapons drill as a warning to NATO to keep clear of the Ukraine conflict. With the confidence of a bully whose bluff is never called, he puffs out his chest and declares to the world: 'We are answering to our thousand-year history and our ancestors . . . We will not allow anyone to threaten us.'

◊

It's not hard, is it, to see where this might be heading. What will the full consequences be this time? But maybe, just maybe, those consequence are already being felt. Maybe the endgame has already begun.

◊

Southwest Israel, 7th October 2023. Hamas gunmen arrived at the Nova music festival near the Re'im kibbutz after breaking through the border fence at 6 a.m. and started shooting the young music lovers. Their mission? 'To kill . . . anyone we saw.' Recordings show them gunning down those fleeing across the desert and shooting into the portable toilet cubicles where others were hiding. It's hard to think of a worse way to die. By the time they moved on to other targets, around 260 festival goers were dead, some raped, others decapitated and otherwise mutilated. Many more were wounded.

At the Be-eri, Kfar Aza and Nir Oz kibbutzim close by, the gunmen entered the perimeters and slaughtered many hundreds more, including children, babies and the elderly. Young military trainees at the nearby Zikim military academy suffered a similar fate. Altogether, eleven military bases were attacked, with four being overrun and their occupants slaughtered. Everywhere they went that morning, the killers seized hostages and dragged them into tunnels on the other side of the border.

It is estimated that more than 1100 people, some of them tourists and guest workers, were killed on that day, and more than 250 kidnapped. Learning of the unexpected success of the attacks, one Palestinian in Gaza City said: 'We were ecstatic. It's like a dream that is hard to wake up from.'

The antisemitic pogrom, banished from the world since the Germans retreated across the Oder in early 1945, had returned.

◊

At 11.35 a.m. that same day, Israeli prime minister Benjamin Netanyahu addressed his nation. 'Citizens of Israel, we are at war . . . The enemy will pay an unprecedented price.' Gaza, he said later, is 'the city of evil . . . We will turn all the places where Hamas is organised and hiding into cities of ruins.'

◊

Netanyahu was true to his word. The bombing began. On 27th May 2024 the world's newspapers carried reports of Red Cross workers collecting burned pieces of dismembered children's bodies from the smouldering remains of a Rafah tent camp in the Gaza Strip following an overnight Israeli airstrike. The camp's Palestinian population had been assured their refuge was safe from attack, but the reality was that no genuine shelter remained in Gaza. This was only the latest incident in Israel's retaliatory offensive: just as dozens of cities were razed and millions killed by aerial bombardment in the six years following the invasion of Poland, Gaza had by this point been flattened and around 36,000 people (the exact numbers are disputed) killed in the eight months following Hamas's brutal incursion.

Not only has the age of pogroms returned, but so too the age of murderous mass retribution and indiscriminate aerial bombing.

◊

Do you ever stop to ask, *'Is it all going to happen again?'*

CONCLUSION

We know where populism can lead: to dictatorship, to Treblinka, to the Gulag, to wars and dead cities. In this struggle to avert the twentieth century's populist disaster from repeating, only history can save us. We need to remaster the past, and quickly, before it reconquers us.

History possesses an immense energy and it lies everywhere around us. We must learn to see that energy, understand it and harness it to save ourselves. Everyone must try.

In a recurring scene in Christopher Nolan's film *Oppenheimer*, the famous nuclear physicist looks not *at* solid objects but *through* them. He sees not the outward form of matter but the energy contained within it, with its frightening power to destroy the world. He feels the need to master that energy, warn the world about it and put it to work for the cause of civilisation. This is what historians – meaning well-informed citizens – must now try to see: not just the present but the past that created and formed the present: a human world constantly changing, expending energy, reshaping its economy, its politics and the lives of human beings: a place of dangerous power that can be controlled only with effort and courage. Just as the physicist sees matter in constant movement, the historian sees time in constant movement. Historians have seen the populists, the dictators, the pogroms, the concentration camps and the bombers appear before, and know they can appear again. But only if we let them.

Consciously or not, and whether we like it or not, we are all in important ways living in the past. It's all around us, embodied in our material and mental worlds. Just look. Earthworks, bricks, steel . . . institutions, constitutions, parties . . . classes, ideologies, habits . . . alliances, animosities, conflict. Like the grooves on a vinyl record, they guide how we think and how we respond to what's going on today. Recognising history gives us an advantage, and a salvation if we want to grasp it.

And grasping it begins in part with recognising that, to those who lived through it, the past looked just like it does today. The temptation is always to see the past in black and white. Not metaphorically, but literally, like in those documentaries about the Second World War played in an endless loop on the History Channel. All that grainy old black-and-white film makes the past seem so different, as if it happened on some other planet to some other species, especially now that the politicians and the generals of those times are long dead. Seeing the conflict in black and white encourages a lie: that only old fools in top hats and winged collars, tweed jackets and woollen ties ever let mass murder and great wars happen. People who look and dress like us couldn't possibly make the same mistake. Or could they?

We need to imagine ourselves back to the times of our grandparents and great-grandparents. To the people of the 1920s and '30s, political events appeared just as they appear to us – in clear, vivid colour. Hitler and Stalin looked frightening, fallible and clownish – just as Trump and Putin do today. The militias threatening the Reichstag in 1933 looked as thuggish as those that threatened the US Capitol in 2021. The sudden arrival of a Nazi death squad in a Jewish Polish village on a sunny day in September 1939 was as terrifying as the arrival of a Hamas death squad in a kibbutz near the Gaza Strip in October 2023. And the bombs that rained down on Guernica were as petrifying as the missiles now crashing into apartment blocks and refugee camps in Kyiv and Gaza. The dead children looked just as dead; their parents' grief felt just as devastating. Only when we grasp this can we truly see that what has happened once can happen again. Indeed, it is happening again.

The psychological climate of Stalin's Soviet Union and Nazi Germany can be felt afresh. In Russia and other places, opponents of the populists again live in fear of a late-night knock on the door, sudden arrest, or murder by some deranged extremist bearing a hammer or knife. Politicians look warily at street crowds, wondering who may be carrying a pistol. Activists ponder whether they will be beaten to death in some remote prison. Punches are thrown in parliaments and street violence is incited to create an atmosphere of chaos, followed by demands for crackdowns to restore order. Flags bearing brutal, feudal symbols appear in public. Can you feel it repeating?

At present, time seems against us. It's all coming back so quickly and our response is cautious, hesitant, lagging. Meanwhile, the naysayers scoff loudly and the populists try constantly to bypass history by substituting dangerous myths for historical truths. But there is hope. If we can recognise destructive patterns as they begin to repeat, we can act decisively and avoid them. As we look at the world today, it's not hard to be terrified. Not long ago, thanks to those who won the Second World War and then had the foresight to bring stability and calmness to the world, we thought the savage, murderous era of the populists was over, never to return. Now that era is coming back. Armed with the insights of history, we have it in our power to stop the populists from destroying our world once again. What practical lessons do those insights provide? I believe there are five.

First, leniency must be reserved for those who deserve it. Populists and dictators must be removed, impeached, prosecuted and jailed when the evidence is there to do so. The law must not hesitate. At dangerous moments in history – moments like now – the law is what stands between us and the noose.

Second, the conditions in which extremists flourish must be addressed. Prolonged periods of inequality and economic discontent are often followed by sudden and devastating economic shocks. As in the Great Depression, this is the moment of democracy's maximum danger. Those whose livelihoods have been destroyed by the remorseless amoral direction of the economy cannot continue to be ignored. Economists cannot continue to regard preserving democracy as everyone else's responsibility – an unfunded externality that politicians alone must absorb. The redistribution of income is no longer a left-wing cause, it is a democratic – even civilisational – imperative.

Third, we must read the signs early, because they are everywhere. Listen to what populist leaders are saying and take note, because sometimes, they really do mean it. Donald Trump said to his followers on the day of the failed coup attempt, 'Our incredible journey is only just beginning.' Hitler couldn't have put it better himself after his coup failed in 1923. It's not over. If not Trump, it could be someone else.

Fourth, arm democracy against populism. Populists only respect strength, so use it against them before you no longer have a choice. Face them on the battlefield while they are still weak enough to defeat. Never back down.

And fifth, rid yourself of the idea that it can't all happen again. The Overton window is a managerial myth – anything is possible, anytime. If in 1989, as the Berlin Wall was coming down, someone had told you that three decades later an armed mob would try to take over the US Congress to overturn a presidential election, you wouldn't have believed it, would you? Or that, for the last two and half decades, Russia would have been ruled not by communists but by fascists? Or that anti-Jewish pogroms would return? Or that there would be a major ground war in Europe again, complete with trenches and tank battles and the mass bombing of cities? Well, it's all happened. What might happen tomorrow, next year, next decade?

◊

If something can happen once, it can happen again. These nine words must become democracy's rallying cry.

POSTSCRIPT

Time advances at double speed . . . another year races by . . . we accelerate further into the past . . .

◊

Thursday 27th June 2024, the Democrat's gerontocratic leader is humiliated in a televised debate, giving the demagogue Trump his opportunity to return . . . Sunday 30th June, Marine Le Pen's far right National Rally and coalition partner combine to win a third of the vote in the first round of a snap election . . . Thursday 4th July, Nigel Farage's Reform party wins 14.3% of the vote – the third highest share – to propel the British populist hard right onto the main stage of British politics . . . They're now even inside the House of Commons . . .

Tuesday 5th November, the Democrats' doomed replacement is, predictably, crushed and on Monday 20th January, having miraculously escaped a lone assassin's bullet, Trump returns to the White House. That evening, at an inauguration rally, his biggest individual donor, Elon Musk, taps his heart with his right hand and lets out a Nazi salute. The next day on X, the Anti-Defamation League calls the action 'an awkward gesture in a moment of enthusiasm, not a Nazi salute' and suggests 'all sides should give one another a bit of grace, perhaps even the benefit of the doubt and take a breath. This is a new beginning.' Not really – at least not to those who know their history . . . Then on Thursday 20th February at CPAC, the demagogue's former campaign manager, the recently released felon Steve Bannon, repeats 'the German greeting' and the ecstatic crowd cheers. History accelerates backwards even faster. We begin to see recurring patterns, but struggle to keep up . . .

The next day, Trump cleans out the military leadership – sacking the Chairman of the Joint Chiefs of Staff (who happens to be black), the Chief of Naval Operations (who happens to be a woman), the Vice Chief of Staff of the Air Force, and the three Judge Advocates General for the Army, Navy and Air Force, who are responsible for enforcing military discipline on anyone who may disobey a presidential order.

A quixotic cabinet of eccentrics and libertarian billionaires is eventually formed to help dismantle the liberal state without congressional approval and maybe gain whatever contracts and kickbacks they can manage . . . The media tycoons surrender at once, donating millions to the president's inauguration fund, paying $40 million for the rights to the First Lady's already very public life story, settling frivolous law suits in Trump's favour, recasting the opinion pages of their once-great newspapers, replacing television news editors, and de-contracting high-rating satirists in order to be admitted to the leader's club . . . (The shakedown is on. How long will it be before, like Hugenberg, the media tycoons will need to crawl into their closets and hide in the woods?)

The dismantling and cleansing of the bureaucracy begins when laptop-armed youths are chaotically set loose inside the leader's most loathed public service departments . . . The round-ups of the undesirables poisoning the blood of the nation follows soon after. First they come for the Latin American immigrants, then the Middle-Eastern ones . . . The deportations follow (this time using aeroplanes instead of trains and resettling in the south not the east) . . . And when people protest, the National Guard and the Marine Corps are sent in their thousands to the streets of San Francisco , then other 'blue' cities, as enforcers . . . The universities are shaken out, the heads of cultural institutions are replaced with philistines whose children – like those of the cowardly media tycoons – may one day despise them for their craven surrender . . . Books are removed from library shelves . . . history begins to be rewritten . . . words are banned from government websites . . . the news we see is manipulated by algorithms . . . the concept of objective truth begins to fade out of the world and lies start to pass into history . . .

Liberals retain their admirable faith in moderation and the rule of law, until the leader's handpicked Supreme Court judges reinterpret the law in new and interesting ways . . .

Then on September 10th 2025, another lone gunman on a rooftop picks up a rifle and with a single shot assassinates one of the MAGA movement's most articulate propagandists and organisers, Charlie Kirk. President Trump and his Vice-President J.D. Vance have no doubt who is to blame – the far left – and promise to go after them hard and dismantle their networks (including, naturally, the Soros Foundation). Steve Bannon says America is at war and needs a steely resolve. Less than three weeks before, White House Deputy Chief of Staff and homeland security adviser Stephen Miller had gone on Fox News and called the Democratic Party a domestic extremist organisation. His wife, the conservative political adviser Katie Miller, says the media and prominent Democratic activists now have blood on their hands. White Supremacist Matt Forney says this is MAGA's Reichstag Fire moment. Journalists and television hosts are sacked and taken off air for refusing to treat Kirk as a martyr. How fast the terror accelerates. Its speed sends its victims into a spin. Like their grandparents' and great-grandparents' generation, they are shocked, smashed, their defences overwhelmed. Organised resistance seems hopeless . . .

Do you ever stop and ask yourself, is it all going to happen again?

◊

In Europe the trench lines solidify. Neither side can gain the knockout blow. The Russian dictator throws conscripts and released prisoners against Ukraine's well-prepared defences to be returned to their mothers in caskets . . . The Ukrainians survive on determination and imported arms, but for how long those arms will keep coming is never easy to say . . . In August 2024 to demonstrate their continuing capacity to fight and win, they cross the Russian border into the Kursk Oblast. By the end of the first week they capture 1,000 square kilometres of territory. Some 79 years earlier, many of their grandparents and great-grandparents fought Hitler's war machine to a standstill on the same spot in the Battle of Kursk. People say history never repeats . . . 'Look,' they tell us, 'it's complicated and uneven and here's a far better metaphor to explain it . . .' They are wrong . . .

Their military demonstration over, the Ukrainians pull back to their border the following March. Has it worked? Will the world continue to help them? The Europeans, maybe having learned from history, stand firm and increase aid and political pressure on Trump and Putin. But there's a problem: in the way that Hitler could admire and cut a deal with Stalin, Trump admires and wants to cut a deal with Putin. The supply of American weapons, approved by Congress, is halted . . . We are back in 1938. And just like in 1938, Trump invites Ukraine's hopeful leader Volodymyr Zelensky to the White House only to humiliate him – the way the British and French humiliated Czechoslovakia's leader Edvard Beneš at Munich. And as the British and French also did at Munich, Trump wants to reward the aggressor by forcing the victim to cede its well-fortified border territories, effectively disarm itself and concede the war – the likely result of which is easy to predict: Zelensky and his ministers will be arrested, given a show trial and shot in one of Stalin's old Arctic prison camps, newly renovated . . .

The Kyiv Blitz begins . . . While the Europeans work hard to convince Trump that Putin can never be trusted, Ukrainians flee nightly to their shelters to escape the hundreds of missiles and drones that nightly rain down . . . Kyiv becomes the new London, the new Hamburg, the new Berlin . . .

On 22nd June 2025, *The Guardian* reports that more than one million Russians and more than 400,000 Ukrainians have been killed or wounded since the war began . . . Yes, 1.4 million casualties . . . By contrast, Hitler's conquest of France cost just 162,000 German casualties and 290,000 French . . .

Do you ever stop and ask – is it all going to happen again?

◊

In Gaza, the killing continues. On both sides, madness completely takes hold . . . The hostages – even their remains – are not released, and the bombs continue to fall, and another new age of savagery descends . . . As in the aerial bombardments of the second world war, abstract thinking replaces concrete realities, with map references instead of homes, potential terrorists instead of civilians, tired and transparent propaganda instead of starving children . . . As the weeks pass, Gaza begins to resemble wartime Guernica, London, Dresden, Warsaw and Tokyo . . . By August 2025 around 1,400 Israelis and 62,000 Palestinians are credibly reported dead in this never-ending war . . .

Gaza's people are effectively under siege and are beginning to starve. Rumours circulate of Israeli plans to resettle them – all of them – to a new camp in the south, amidst the ruins of Rafah, where they will be housed, fed and policed at their captors' mercy, likely where the world's press can't easily report on what's going on, before being forcefully deported across the world . . .

So here we are again, back in the past . . . Our grandparents' and great-grandparents' past . . . And, living in this past, is it any wonder the language we gradually, though reluctantly, reach for to describe it is the one our grandparents and great-grandparents used? A language with words like populism, fascism, appeasement, moral savagery, area bombing, concentration camps, ghettos, deportations, crimes against humanity, genocide and more . . .

◊

So . . . *Do you ever stop and ask, "Is it all going to happen again?"*

◊

The mistakes of the 1920s and '30s are being repeated. If a third world war develops, it is likely already in its early stages, just as the election of the Nazis and the first pogroms against the Jews and the invasions of Manchuria and Abyssinia and the bombing of Guernica and the Munich disaster can said to be the early stages of the second world war . . . Maybe the question that confronts us now is this: Can we stop the casualty count from this new era of conflict from reaching that of the second world war? And, given the widespread availability of nuclear weapons, can we stop the casualty count exceeding it, many times over? Can we stop the populists and the madness before it's too late?

◊

If there is hope it lies in the past.

In October 1962, U.S. President John F. Kennedy had to decide how to respond to the Soviet placement of nuclear missiles on Cuba. Over thirteen days, he came under intense pressure from hawkish members of the Joint Chiefs of Staff to use air strikes to destroy the Soviet missiles on the ground. Could he get the missiles removed without causing Armageddon?

Kennedy found his inspiration in a recently published history book. In 1962 Barbara Tuchman, a non-academic historian with a gift for dramatic and epic storytelling, published *The Guns of August*. It told in narrative form, how in 1914 the old order that had ruled Europe for centuries had committed suicide by stumbling into the first world war through a series of catastrophic miscalculations. In his account of the tense events of the Cuban crisis, the President's principal speechwriter and later White House historian Ted Sorensen, told of how Kennedy spoke openly of the lessons to be gained from Tuchman's book. The mistakes of the past, Kennedy thought, could – and must – be avoided. Secretary of State Robert S. McNamara recounted similarly. On the tenth day of the stand-off, Sorensen attended a meeting at which the President said his aim was to avoid doing things that would cause someone in the future to write a book like Tuchman's called *The Missiles of October*. The scene is dramatically presented in the Kevin Costner 2000 film *Thirteen Days*.

When it was released, professional historians roundly dismissed *The Guns of August* for its lack of necessary academic rigour. The public, though, loved it and it won the Pulitzer Prize for General Non-Fiction in 1963, staying on the *New York Times* bestseller list for 42 weeks. By helping save the world from nuclear war, *The Guns of August* can credibly be called the most important history book ever written. Citizen-historians like Barbara Tuckman and John F. Kennedy are needed once again. To find one, simply look in the mirror.

Only history can save us.

ACKNOWLEDGEMENTS

Repeat has been on my mind every day since Donald Trump's attempted insurrection in January 2021. It is an important and urgent story and I would like to thank the publishers, editors and marketing teams at Black Inc. and Allison & Busby for helping me tell it.

Like all my writing, this book was inspired and developed in discussion with a wide circle of brilliant friends who share my concerns about the perilous state of democracy and freedom and the need to act. Their most important quality? Not their willingness to agree but, rather, their compulsion to probe, question, disagree and point me in new directions – the very qualities we need in these dangerous times when free speech is in deep peril. I have thanked them personally already. You know who you are!

I would also like to express my gratitude to the many historians, political journalists and public intellectuals whose writings I have consulted. Conceived as a polemic aimed at a popular audience, *Repeat: A Warning from History* has intentionally avoided academic footnoting, but where I have borrowed arguments, I have endeavoured to acknowledge this in the body of my narrative. A full list of sources consulted is attached in the section 'Further Reading'.

Lastly, a concluding word for us citizen-historians. They say that history is always written by the victors. This is too passive. We must think of it another way: *Historians make victory possible*. Their lessons are democracy's best weapons. Time to put them to use.

FURTHER READING

To tell this story, I have used the following books, literary magazines and newspaper articles.

John Maynard Keynes and the Paris Peace Treaty

John Maynard Keynes, *The Economic Consequences of the Peace* (Macmillan, 1971, originally published 1919)

Margaret MacMillan, *Paris 1919: Six Months that Changed the World* (John Murray, 2001)

Robert Skidelsky, *John Maynard Keynes: Hopes Betrayed 1888–1920* (Viking, 1986)

Robert Skidelsky, *John Maynard Keynes: Fighting for Britain 1937–1946* (Macmillan, 2000)

The rise of Adolf Hitler

Richard J. Evans, *The Coming of the Third Reich* (Penguin, 2004)

Richard J. Evans, *The Third Reich in Power* (Penguin, 2006)

Mark Jones, *1923: The Forgotten Crisis in the Year of Hitler's Coup* (Basic Books, 2023)

Ian Kershaw, *Hitler 1889–1936: Hubris* (Penguin, 1999)

Laurence Rees, *The Nazis: A Warning from History* (BBC Books, 1997)

Timothy W. Ryback, *Takeover: Hitler's Final Rise to Power* (Headline, 2024)

Timothy Snyder, *Bloodlands: Europe Between Hitler and Stalin* (Basic Books, 2010)

Volker Ullrich, *Hitler: Ascent, 1889–1939* (Knopf, 2016)

Volker Weidermann, *Dreamers: When the Writers Took Power, Germany 1918* (Pushkin Press, 2018)

Christopher Isherwood

Christopher Isherwood, *Christopher and His Kind* (Vintage Books, 2012, originally published 1976)

Christopher Isherwood, *Goodbye to Berlin* (Vintage Books, 1998, originally published 1939)

Peter Parker, *Isherwood: A Life Revealed* (Random House, 2004)

Joseph Stalin's Soviet Union

M.T. Anderson, *Symphony for the City of the Dead: Dmitri Shostakovich and the Siege of Leningrad* (Candlewick Press, 2015)

Christopher Andrew & Oleg Gordievsky, *KGB: The Inside Story* (Hodder & Stoughton, 1990)

Orlando Figes, *Revolutionary Russia, 1891–1991: A History* (Pelican, 2014)

Osip Mandelstam, *Selected Poems*, trans. Clarence Brown & W.S. Merwin (Penguin, 1977)

Aleksandr Solzhenitsyn, *The Gulag Archipelago 1918–1956* (Book Club Associates, 1974)

D.M. Thomas, *Alexander Solzhenitsyn: A Century in His Life* (Little, Brown and Company, 1998)

The Spanish Civil War

Antony Beevor, *The Battle for Spain: The Spanish Civil War 1936–1939* (Weidenfeld & Nicolson, 2006)

George Orwell

On Fascist rallies

George Orwell, *Animal Farm* (Secker & Warburg, 1945)

George Orwell, '*Road to Wigan Pier* Diaries', *Collected Works*, Vol. X, pp.456–57 (Secker & Warburg, 2002)

On the similarities between fascism and communism

George Orwell, 'Review of *Assignment in Utopia* by Eugene Lyons', *Collected Works*, Vol. XI, pp.158–60 (Secker & Warburg, 2002)

George Orwell, 'Review of *The Totalitarian Enemy* by F. Borkenau', *Collected Works*, Vol. XII, pp.158–60 (Secker & Warburg, 2002)

On the decision to fight

George Orwell, 'My country right or left', *Collected Works*, Vol. XII, pp.269–72 (Secker & Warburg, 2002)

W.H. Auden

Ian Sansom, *September 1, 1939: W.H. Auden and the Afterlife of a Poem* (Fourth Estate, 2019)

Second World War deaths

The Oxford Companion to World War II (Oxford University Press, 2005), p.225

The postwar economic and political settlement

Eric Hobsbawm, *The Age of Extremes: The Short Twentieth Century 1914–1991* (Abacus, 1995)

Tony Judt, *Ill Fares the Land* (Allen Lane, 2010)

Tony Judt, *Postwar: A History of Europe Since 1945* (Vintage, 2010, originally published 2005)

Andrew Leigh, *The Shortest History of Economics* (Black Inc., 2024)

George Packer, *The Unwinding: Thirty Years of American Decline* (Faber & Faber, 2013)

Thomas Piketty, *Capital in the Twenty-First Century* (Harvard University Press, 2014)

Vladimir Putin's Russia

Svetlana Alexievich, *Secondhand Time: The Last of the Soviets* (Text Publishing, 2016)

Christian Caryl, 'Mourning Navalny', *The New York Review of Books*, 4 April 2024

Robyn Dixon, 'Under Putin, a militarized new Russia rises to challenge U.S. and the West', *The Washington Post*, 7 May 2024

Orlando Figes, *A People's Tragedy: The Russian Revolution 1891–1924* (Pimlico, 1997)

Sheila Fitzpatrick, *The Shortest History of the Soviet Union* (Black Inc., 2022)

Masha Gessen, 'Art is now a crime in Russia', *The New Yorker*, 9 May 2023

The Guardian, 'Russia adds writer Boris Akunin to terrorist list over criticism of war', *The Guardian*, 19 December 2023

Michael Mainville, 'Yegor Gaidar obituary', *The Guardian*, 17 December 2009

'Putin sits at the heart of the West's illiberal axis', *The Washington Post*, 7 May 2024

Trudy Rubin, 'The biggest story last week was not Stormy Daniels or campus protests', *The Philadelphia Inquirer*, 12 May 2024

The rise of Donald Trump and the alt-right

ABC News, 'Donald Trump 2.0: This is what the former president says he'll do if he wins the 2024 US election', 21 March 2024

Isaac Arnsdorf, 'How Steve Bannon guided the MAGA movement's rebound from Jan. 6', *The Washington Post*, 4 April 2024

Jelani Cobb, 'After Bannon', *The New Yorker*, 4 September 2017

Fernanda Eberstadt, 'Pranksters into prophets', *The Times Literary Supplement*, No. 5807, 18 July 2014

Final Report of the Select Committee to Investigate the January 6th Attack on the United States Capitol, US Government Publishing Office, 22 December 2022

Adam Gabbatt, 'Golden escalator ride: The surreal day Trump kicked off his bid for president', *The Guardian*, 15 June 2019

Lloyd Green, 'That's Hitler, Bannon thought', *The Guardian*, 11 December 2022

Andrew Marantz, 'The illiberal order', *The New Yorker*, 4 July 2022

Chris Michael and agencies, 'Trump says he will be a dictator only on 'day one' if elected president', *The Guardian*, 6 December 2023

Chris Michael, 'Trump tells rally immigrants are 'poisoning the blood of our country'', *The Guardian*, 17 December 2023

Speech by Prime Minister Viktor Orbán at the opening of the CPAC Hungary conference, April 25, 2024, Budapest

Tess Owen, "Far-right commentators echo Trump in calling for 'vengeance and retribution' for Charlie Kirk's death", *The Guardian*, 12 September 2025

Martin Pengelly, 'Rupert Murdoch often wishes Donald Trump dead, Michael Wolff book says', *The Guardian*, 20 September 2023

Martin Pengelly, "Elon Musk appears to make back-to-back fascist salutes at inauguration rally", *The Guardian*, 21 January 2025

Victor Sebestyen, "Bannon says he's a Leninist: that could explain the White House's new tactics", *The Guardian*, 7 February 2017

Emma Shortis, 'Friday essay: Project 2025 . . .', *The Conversation*, 26 April 2024

William Thomas, 'You will not replace us', *The New Yorker*, 4 December 2017

Elisabeth Zerofsky, 'The illiberal state', *The New Yorker*, 14 January 2019

The war in Ukraine

Serhii Plokhy, *The Russo-Ukrainian War* (Penguin, 2023)

The war in Gaza

Daniel Boffey and Sam Jones, "Israel's darkest day: the 24 hours of terror that shook the country", *The Guardian*, 14 October 2023

DENNIS GLOVER was educated at Monash and Cambridge universities and has made a career as one of Australia's leading political speechwriters. He is the author of several fiction and non-fiction works. His first novel, *The Last Man in Europe*, which tells the dramatic story of George Orwell's struggle to write *Nineteen Eighty-Four*, was published around the world and listed for several major literary prizes, including the Walter Scott Prize for Historical Fiction. He lives in Melbourne with his partner and two children.

www.dennisglover.net